FIELD
N❦TES

FIELD NOTES

A Geography of Mourning

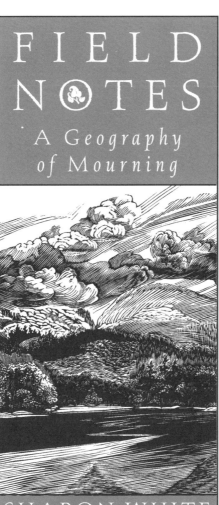

SHARON WHITE

HAZELDEN®

Hazelden
Center City, Minnesota 55012-0176

1-800-328-0094
1-651-213-4590 (Fax)
www.hazelden.org

Library of Congress Cataloging-in-Publication Data

White, Sharon.
    Field notes : a geography of mourning / Sharon White.
      p. cm.
    ISBN 1-56838-878-0 softcover
    1. Bereavement—Psychological aspects. 2. White,
  Sharon. 3. Widows—Biography. I. Title.
    BF575.G7 W485 2002
    155.9'37'092—dc21
    [B]

                                                      2002068643

06 05 04 03 02   6 5 4 3 2 1

Cover design by David Spohn
Interior design by David Spohn
Typesetting by Stanton Publication Services, Inc.

For my parents

Contents

Acknowledgments

Special thanks to Chris Jerome for her generous help and encouragement from the very beginning through the end of this project; to Maddy Blais, Karen Donovan, and Kit Ward for conversations and comments on my work; to Mary Fenn, my guide through Brownsville's history; to my agent, Linda Roghaar, for her perseverance; and to Richard Solly, my editor.

1

*For thousands of miles my chief converse has been
in the wilderness with the spontaneous production of nature;
and the study of these objects and their contemplation
has been to me a source of constant delight.*
THOMAS NUTTALL, *North American Sylva*

The pipes are frozen this morning. I'm up before the light trying to thaw them and this early morning work has made me think of other things. How long grief lasts, how the earth always extends as far as you want it to. How my geography stretches out from where I am and seems expansive here where I can see basins and ranges moving.

Each morning I find my way back to the day before and hope that I haven't lost ground. Each day I remember who I am after months of concentrating on each step.

Here in Kelly, Wyoming, the cottonwoods bristle out in uneven branches to this pure winter cold. Dried sage shoots out and buds. The tracks of elk and moose lead to the river. I can count the elements that surround me. Snow piles up around the slim stems of wheat-colored flowers.

Yesterday I kicked through snow and frozen grasses across the fields to the general store. It was closed but the owner, a small woman wrapped in a coat inside the cold store, let me in. I found a week-old *Denver Post*. "We only get them on weekends," she told me. I rummaged through the shelves for something to eat.

When I put a can of tomato soup on the counter, she said, "We're low this time of year." And when she saw the kind of crackers I picked out she nodded, "These are good." She turned the box for the price. "We had them last night."

LAST SUMMER, a year after my husband's death, when I was riding a bus across the island of Skye in Scotland, I thought about how one pain often cancels another. Loneliness and cold can take away the sharpness of grief. The landscape there, the green, bare hills with one house painted white here and there, one woman running to the bus, and the ocean moving under me could all extend the edge of my mind to the world.

The silence of Wyoming seems to come from a long, long time ago. You hear it in the light, in the wind-twisted tree, in the river washing over green stones, in the prints of rabbits, in the castellated mountains rising to the north. It stretches out all along the basin and comes into my heart where I sit watching the morning. Each word I write sheds days, the sentences reach into months and the pages extend, tracing backwards into the disorder of syllables.

I think it's the water pump that's frozen. I have the stove roaring, incinerating pine logs—two heaters going and nothing seems to be happening. Ted, a friend who moved to Wyoming a few years ago, has given me the gift of his home while he's in Alaska. I call Don Kent, his landlord, and find out I was supposed to keep the water running, "even if it's only a trickle," all night. I had been afraid of that.

The sun isn't going to show. At least not yet; there's a milky sky. Weather reports. The last two years I've kept weather reports on my brain. How does it look? Lots of clouds? Bit of rain, imminent snowstorm? Avalanche? I take the pulse of each current that runs from what is happening to who I am.

I check the view from the east window. A tall weed rocks in the morning wind, balancing against air. I think these are aspens, not cottonwoods. Bristly-looking aspens. Black crows float into the trees, calling out to each other. Fences position themselves with small drama across the sage-broken land. The sky turns pink.

"Sure, it's beautiful, but when you've lived here your whole life and you have to do things in this weather, you forget what it looks like," the plumber tells me. He has come with Mr. Kent to thaw the pipes. "But then I go away, and when I come back I have to say that no place ever looks as pretty."

They give me ski reports (lousy, rocks, long waits), advice on where to go running (up the road over the bridge through the subdivision), and crucial information that I still don't have straight on how to keep the pipes from freezing again. Does hot water run in the bathroom or the kitchen?

"There are moose all over the place, you just have to look for them," Don Kent tells me. "I saw one down by the river along the highway yesterday morning."

I tell them about the big tracks I saw, and they think for a minute they might be Teton Ranch cows, but then remember that the owner keeps them penned in the winter. There's soil, they tell me, that blows over from Idaho and settles on the tops of buttes near here. The soil looks like perfect loam but won't hold water. A fellow has been trying to make a pond up there for years but has had no luck.

TODAY IS MY BIRTHDAY. I woke early and lit the stove. As I ate breakfast, I watched the figures move from their homes to cars and trucks parked in the field. One figure in a long red coat raced around the side of his cabin and dashed to his truck. Another, a woman in a long skirt and long woolen coat, walked across the sage-studded field to the cabin that faces me to the west.

I am trying to live in the here and now. The typewriter is cold. The map hangs on the wall, the stove sits to my left. I drink tea with lots of milk. Here the details are all trimmed down. And with this shaving away I see farther. The full moon overnight, in the early hours of January 3rd, returned me to that January 3rd two years ago when we found out Steve had a brain tumor. He died in early April. He was thirty-three years old. We had been married one and a half years.

That day had been my birthday, too. I was counting on some sort of luck because there was a lineup of threes. The third of January, my thirty-third birthday. My father arrived suddenly to drive us to Dr. Bobowick's office. I don't remember the weather. I don't remember getting into the car.

When the doctor finished his examination of Steve, we moved from the examining room into his office. "Well," he said, "you did very well with the memory exercises and motor skills. But the results of the CAT scan were not good.

There's a shadow. Dr. Chan, who has a lot of experience reading these scans, thinks it's probably a tumor."

Steve was sitting at the side of Dr. Bobowick's desk and I was next to him in a white chair. Suddenly the chair was leaning back and Steve was saying, "It's okay honey. Everything is going to be all right."

And Dr. Bobowick handed me little foil packets filled with tranquilizers that sat unopened in my pocket for months until I threw them away.

THE LIGHT COMES into my bones somehow here, reminding me I have blood and tissue and sinew. Surrounded by cold and quiet, I suddenly understand just what I'm made of. The fire burns, shifting each liquid ember to coal. I wonder if the car will start and how cold it is outside and whether I'll see a moose today.

I run up the road above town, circling past large, new houses perched on a ridge. As I run, I remember the heavy tan boots we bought Steve. I see him struggling to get his feet into those boots before we drove to the hospital in Waterbury, Connecticut—the hospital where I was born—for his radiation treatments. He would lie on a table I refused to look at. When it was over, he would grab his red hat from the rack and I'd fold up my magazine, and we would grope our way along the rail to the elevator.

We stayed with my parents in the house they built when I was twelve. Dr. Piscatelli, our family doctor, pointed us in the right direction after Steve and I visited him in December. He knew something was very wrong. Steve's diagnosis followed months of confusion. We had recently moved to western Massachusetts from Colorado, but Steve's new job was not working out. I had no idea that we would only live together in the cottage in Leeds for less than a month before Steve became too sick to work.

Sometimes no one knew where he was. When I asked him, he couldn't remember where he had been.

He had visited a doctor at the Veterans Administration Hospital down the street from our house in Massachusetts. The doctor told him he was just depressed. A doctor in Aspen had given him the same diagnosis months before.

"Have you ever felt confused like this before?" I asked Steve as we walked a loop of paved streets near our house.

"Yes, when I moved to Denver."

"This is not," Dr. Piscatelli would later say, "the kind of man who gets depressed."

We had no health insurance. The hospital in Connecticut offered to cover Steve's care for free. I conferred with several doctors, and no one was sure how long Steve would live. One doctor offered to perform brain surgery for free, but no one seemed to know if this would help. The operation, the doctors told me, would probably not be successful.

Instead, we decided on an operation in which a shunt was inserted to drain off the fluid that was collecting. Steve's doctor thought the procedure would improve his condition. After the shunt was in place, it was visible on the side of his head. It looked like a pencil-sized tube that traced a line down to his neck.

A team of doctors operated on Steve at the VA hospital in New Haven. The head surgeon looked very young to me.

"If you want someone with gray hair," he told me, "you'll have to get someone else."

A different doctor, Dr. Dickey, was in charge of Steve's care. He told my father, but not me, that Steve would live three months. This was in January. He died on April 9th.

When the operation was over, Steve seemed better. In intensive care he kissed me like the first time we kissed, on a dark street in a bad section of Denver. His mother, who had arrived from Iowa, wiped the walls around his bed with Lysol. I played a kind of crazy scrabble with Steve. Our rules were that any kind of word, even if it wasn't a word, was okay. One day Steve and I stood looking out a window at the horizon and he said, "I'll never see the ocean again, will I."

I said, "Oh, of course you will. When we get out of this place, I'll take you there."

At night I could hear Joyce, Steve's mother, weeping on the other side of the wall in my brother's old bedroom.

After a week we wheeled him out of the hospital.

My parents' house became my house once again. Steve and I drove each morning to St. Mary's for radiation treatments. There was a good chance, the doctors told me, that this could help shrink the tumor. Friends and acquaintances offered other methods of healing.

"You have to do the thinking for Steve," a man who had survived a brain tumor and several bouts of cancer told me. "You have to will him well, since he can't do it for himself."

I bought dried seaweed and brewer's yeast to counteract the side effects of his radiation treatments. I read books about laughter and healing.

Each night my mother cooked us dinner. My brother drove us to New Haven for our weekly visits to Dr. Dickey because I was too upset to drive. During the afternoon, Steve sat in the family room switching the channels of the TV or sleeping. Together, we watched the space shuttle *Challenger* blow up on the screen. We were eating lunch. The sound was off.

One morning in February, Steve looked out of the window of the room I had slept in all through high school and asked, "Why is there ice on the trees in June?" Sometimes Steve would look at the framed photographs of my brother and sister in the living room and not know who they were.

In early March, my parents went to Florida for vacation. After Steve's radiation treatments were finished, I put him on a plane to visit his family in Iowa. My doctor had told me that I needed a rest, but I was reluctant to send Steve off alone. I knew he had a hard time remembering where he was and what he was doing. I felt like I was the only one who could take care of him.

In the airport he went into the men's room and didn't come out for a long time. I was afraid I had missed him and he was wandering the airport, lost. I finally asked someone to watch the door for me while I went inside to look for Steve. I had a hard time convincing him he should come out.

Steve's brother met him in Chicago and they traveled to Iowa together. I went to Florida for a week; after that I was planning to meet Steve in Iowa.

When I called him, he said, "I miss you desperately."

"Is Brenda there?" I asked.

"Yes," he said. "I don't feel great. I feel tired. Sometimes there are too many people all talking yap, yap, yap at the same time."

I RUN UNDER the big sign for the Teton Valley Ranch up the road past moose tracks, along the bristly cottonwoods and spruce. I startle a flock of dark birds on the river and try to run farther than yesterday. The reach of these high plains balances me. The sweep of sage to the river's edge, the old cottonwoods farther on up the road. Flashy mountain crows.

It snows at four. The bodies of birds glance off the edges of the light. The mountains are obscured for the first time in days. Gary, who lives in a canvas yurt at the far end of the field, runs around the cabins and tosses a white plastic bag in his car. His dog jumps in, and they drive off.

I am lonely. I am fingering the edges of books and pacing the length of the trailer. The wind has changed, the clouds have come down. The light grows white, and I pull down into those cluttered places where all the pain hatches itself and festers, and festers.

Fiction is the farthest thing from my mind. The plains stretch out under the light snow to a flatness they didn't have before, and when I wake from a nap, I wonder who I am. Where I came from. How long I've been here.

Where is the heart, I wonder. Who took the heart and planted it in the white soil and covered it with sage. How do I spell heart. Where is my mind; who took the mind and hung it in a room where the king lives, hung it shining like the millions of swords he has hanging from the ceiling above his bed. Swords like broken branches, widow makers, hanging in the crooks of trees.

But then again, there's the snow, isn't there, falling very slowly to the ground to the steps where I need to pile more wood.

WHEN STEVE WAS DYING in the hospital in Iowa City, I used to cross the Mississippi twice a day on my drive from a friend's house in Rock Island, Illinois, to Iowa. I would cross the murky river and watch the green buds grow into new leaves each day, and each day I would say to myself—you will survive this.

Things are simpler if you only have four things to do in the day—wake up, eat breakfast, pile wood, sleep. Once you add going to the store or washing the dishes or walking along the river, things become much more interesting but much harder to control. After all, you may leave the door to the store open, the cold air will race in, a woman will yell, "Why didn't you shut the door?" Your nose may freeze up on the walk, you could burn your hand washing dishes, you may have to talk to someone and answer questions and look into their eyes. You may see the hot breath of horses hang in the cold air.

HOW THE WINDOW joins itself to the wall interests me. The nails and bolts. Shelter. In Wyoming, shelter is often just a wall of lodgepole pines, straight and smooth against the cold. In *American Log Homes* Arthur Thiede and Cindy Teipner write:

Jackson, Wyoming has a heritage of log building that reaches back to its founding in 1897. With vast amounts of lodgepole pine nearby, most early buildings were constructed of logs. Because lodgepole pines tend to grow in dense stands, they are usually very straight, uniform in size, and possess few limbs. These qualities make the species ideal for log building.

It's been twenty degrees below zero here for five days and the wind makes it even colder. In this trailer I feel the outside press against the inside in an amazing and wonderful way. I suppose if I had less wood and no electricity I wouldn't like it as much as I do, but for now it reminds me that we exist like all other animals by finding warmth and food and shelter.

Back East, where I live and work for most of the year, I fend off everything with objects—wedding gifts, furniture from my aunts and my parents, blankets from my sister, paintings from my sister-in-law, electric frying pans from my brother, books, walls, plants, cars. I want to strip my life so I can count the elements once more. So I can hear and see and taste.

Here, I feel as though I could walk across the globe with ease. I am not tied to the cottage in Leeds, Massachusetts, with the heavy wood door, its knocker like a hand, or to the dark classroom where I teach. Here, it's the way the earth tilts, the sage clusters to snow, the moose breathes, the ravens preen or sit motionless on fence posts.

I've closed up the red cottage where the empty branches of black walnut trees lean over the roof and the memory of

Steve walking into the house follows me. I am shedding words. I am shedding connections to the past. I am shedding pain.

When Mr. Kent was here I asked him about the log cabin to the west of the trailer. "Oh, we brought that down from the hill, one of the first homestead cabins around here," he told me. He seemed amused that I was interested.

I can see two other log buildings from these northeast windows. One is another homesteader cabin, rough hewn, dark brown pine chinked with gray mud, the other a large house with a television antenna, flat hewn and grayer. Beyond the two houses are the plains, broken by fences, the sturdy sage, a cottonwood here and there, and along the stream beds, clumps of aspens. The light and the quiet are softened by clouds, by the few inches of snow that fell last night.

I, too, am softened by these watching days. Perhaps here I can sort out the past year and a half in this place where I have no past, no history.

ISN'T THERE ANYTHING FUNNY about this whole thing that you could write about, a man in my dreams asks me. Oh, lots of things, I reply, for instance, when they put it in, when they put the brain tumor in Steve's head, it was funny.

Healing takes a serpentine route. My dreams mend lately. Everyone is whole, there are reasons for things going wrong, babies are beautiful and healthy. Everyone is in love.

All along there were different ways the story could have ended. First it could have been that we just didn't get along; after all, that happens. Or it could have been, as one doctor in Aspen told us, that it was just stress. Or maybe I had an affair and went off traveling. Or he had encephalitis and then everything was fixed with the help of drugs. Or he was clinically depressed and again drugs did the trick. We never thought it would be something as insurmountable as an inoperable brain tumor, an inoperable brain tumor that was very large, as large as my hand held open.

The trailer this morning is warm. It snowed about an inch last night. I consider going out early to look for moose. A *Field Guide to the Mammals* tells me:

> Alces alces *Identification: Height 5–6 1/2 ft. (152–198 cm). Wt.: males, 850–1180 lb. (382.5–531 kg); females 600–800 lb. (270–360 kg). Record antler spread 77 5/8 in. (197 cm). A large dark brown animal with gray legs. By its* large size, overhanging snout, *and pendent* "bell" *on throat, as well as its ungainly appearance, it may be distinguished from all other mammals. . . . Skull has 32 teeth. There are 4 mammae. . . . Habits: . . . Occurs singly or by twos (cow or calf) or threes (bull, cow, calf), rarely in small groups. Browses on many woody plants in winter, twigs, bark, saplings; feeds primarily on aquatic vegetation in summer. Males shed antlers mostly Dec.–Feb. . . . Voice, seldom heard, low* moo *with upward inflection at the end, also low grunts. . . . Can swim as fast as 2 men can paddle a canoe; speeds up to 35 mph (56 kmph) on land. Populations of 4 per sq. mi. (259 ha) are high. Lives 20 years or more in wild.*

I have a notion that the large animal is more elusive than I want to admit. Why would the moose hang around for me to watch him drink from the river or sniff the air? Where do moose sleep? How do they keep warm when it's thirty below? What conversations do they have with themselves? Good grass there, stop now, sleep, where is my mate?

After so many days of intense cold, this warmth, just a few degrees warmer, is a gift. My strength is a gift too. When Steve first died I had a hard time getting out of bed. I could hardly put the kettle on to boil. I took short walks with a friend who was thirty-nine and pregnant with her first child. We walked slowly around a loop where I later taught myself to run again. I had a hard time going out to the garden in the backyard and planting. Each movement of my body was pain. It was pain that, after all, I had survived.

After Steve's dad died less than two months after our wedding, he wanted to buy a star and name it Rex after his father. He wanted to give this to his mother for Christmas. I think we both forgot about it. It was forty dollars which seemed cheap for a star but expensive for us. So we bought her a popcorn popper for fifteen dollars instead of the star. When Steve died I thought about those stars again.

Steve left me slowly. He left me before he knew he was leaving, before I knew he was leaving. One night after we had moved east from Aspen I woke up at two o'clock. Steve was sleeping. I had never felt so alone. I knew something was happening but couldn't figure out what it was. My husband was sleeping; the house kept out the cold. But time stretched ahead of me and I couldn't know where we were going.

I first met Steve in the room where he slept and worked at his drawing table, in a red stone house on a ridge above the Platte River in Denver. He was the art director of *The Bloomsbury Review*. He worked for two or three other publishers to support himself while he built up the book review magazine he founded with a friend.

When I met him, he had just given away the battery in his car to a man who used to live under the viaducts in Denver. He spent an hour each day playing video games at the corner store with a group of neighborhood kids. His thumb was taped up.

I was sure he was in love with a woman he was teaching design to. I had volunteered to work on his magazine, and I'd see him leaning over the light table examining her work when I delivered proofed articles to his room.

But one Saturday, Steve and I spent the morning wrapping magazines in brown paper and bundling them in packages to take to the post office. The man who used to live under the viaducts was there too, and we all argued about gun control. When I left, I knew my life was about to change.

I rode my bike down the paved path along the Platte River until I turned and followed Cherry Creek home. It was October and the whole city of Denver was shimmering with yellow leaves. I had never felt so happy.

"What are your passions?" Steve asked me on our first date. A friend gave him free tickets to a Barbra Streisand movie, and afterward we went out for coffee at a place where there were paintings he wanted to see.

I'd been living in Denver for a few years but never saw

the city until I walked through its neighborhoods with Steve. He took me to a ridge above the Platte where some of the oldest houses in Denver faced the city below. I felt as if I had never been in a place quite like the one I was standing in with him, late at night looking out over the red stone buildings and the wide river and its creeks in electric light.

I think about Steve's passions as I wash my cup and plate after breakfast and add a log to the stove.

He loved the Denver Broncos, his book magazine, conversations about work, the ocean, strange inventions and business operations, the movement of his pen on thin paper, the elegance of words, the shape of vowels on the page, the order of design, his difficult friends, his family, the artists he encouraged and pushed. He never backed down, or gave up, or panicked even when he was dying. He was generous and brave and stubborn. I felt completely loved when he was alive. With his death, I'm not sure who I am.

Sometimes I feel as if Steve has taken me away with him, and I can't find the path through the woods home.

I walk over to the post office at ten and buy a stamp. I remember a man I met in Dominica one spring who hired a young boy from the village as his rabbit feeder.

"I have the boy come," he told me, "because I live alone, you know, and I could break a leg or get sick and no one would know—no one comes from the village to visit—so I keep four rabbits and the boy comes to feed them every day."

I use the postmaster as my rabbit boy. Buy one stamp today, two tomorrow.

"Ted's gone?" he asked yesterday.

"Yep, I'm here," I said and picked up Ted's second-class mail.

Today I scuff my way across the pasture past the cluster of yurts to the post office, another log building. Already I invent a rhythm.

Lee Donaldson, the postmaster, tells me to ski up above the school. "You're my only source of information around here," I tell him and he smiles.

I park Ted's car near the Teton Science School and ski on a forest road that leads up a ditch above the river. On the way back I follow what looks like moose tracks on top of old ski tracks near a place where I thought I heard something on the way out. As I come around the bending trail, I see a moose lightly flying up the hillside, soft brown, shaggy and then two others on the same bank. I see where they've been browsing on willow brush and alder. They stand quietly, just tilting their heads, waiting, I suppose, for me to clear out.

They aren't as big as I imagined. I'm right down where they were browsing so I turn around and ski across the hillside to where I can see their brown shapes through the aspens. On the hill I see their tracks again and places where they've slept: the low bushes, sage nibbled near where the snow is pounded down. On the drive back to Kelly I see two big-eared heads sticking up from the sage in the plains that stretch out to the mountains.

Home, the night comes beyond the window. I hear moose breathe and the ducks along the river settle in. The large crow watches me. I know the snow settles inch by inch along the branches of the alder brush and the red willow clusters and spreads up north from here. The river moves in its slow way along the plains, ditched there for the cows who graze as the night comes down.

Ted tells me over the phone how to work the thermostat, but I can't remember how to do it. I gauge the cold by the frost on the windows or on whether I can see my breath when I wake up in the morning. I've turned the faucets off thinking it's warm enough and I hope I've guessed right.

STEVE'S MOTHER WANTED his body cremated, and like his father's cremated body, put in an urn and then into a niche in a mortuary not far from her house.

In Tibet, according to Ted, who has watched the ceremony, bodies are given a sky burial. They are brought to a place near a cliff where the sky-takers cut the body into pieces and ravens come down to eat the flesh. After most of the body is gone, the bones are burnt and the ashes are given to the family after the sky burial is over. Somehow that seems better than burning the body in a building where the air has to be camouflaged with perfume.

When Steve's father died in the hospital in Des Moines, they were waiting for us. We had taken a short walk, and the doctors wanted Steve to see his father once more before they took the pieces of his body he had willed as organ transplants. We watched Steve's father dying for days, and when he finally died only his wife was with him.

I decided to bury Steve in the graveyard in Iowa near where he had grown up. It seemed easier to think about him buried in the earth. I couldn't imagine ashes. Steve as ashes. No Steve anywhere but in a handful of bones and ashes. Later it would haunt me.

TWO YEARS AGO in early January, I went to Dr. Piscatelli and asked him what Steve's chances were. And he said less than one percent. I held on to that one percent. He had given me the facts but left a small opening of one percent. A crack in the door I kept seeing, hoping we would squeeze through somehow.

When I was little my grandmother used to tell me that if I put a scarf over my head, I would fall away into a dark, deep hole. I thought about this the other day when I was buried in snow up to my neck. I was skiing and had fallen on a steep slope covered with two feet of new powder. One of my skis was caught at an angle to my body and the other was free. I panicked. I thought of how it must feel to be caught in an avalanche and remembered the warning of my grandmother.

It has snowed here for days and this is the first clearing in almost a week. The blue horizon brushes itself again along the tops of the buttes to the east. The mind corners itself sometimes in weather like this, half buried in snow, covered with scarves. There's no way out except to relax, slowly pull your head up from the deep powder, dig your leg out with your hands, and pull and pull.

This past year and a half I have been hitting pockets of snow. Places where I thought I couldn't move. Where I could hardly breathe and I was hanging face down on a mountain. One of those places was thinking of Steve in the shower.

Steve had what the doctors assumed was his first seizure in the shower at my parents' house. And each time I stood under the beating water I would think of the color of Steve's skin when I found him in the shower.

With time I worked myself out of that image. With time all thoughts work themselves into warnings and then into stories.

The mountains are still obscured with clouds.

A FEW YEARS AGO, before Steve got sick, I went for a hike in the mountains with Ted. As we walked up a mining road, I talked about ski trips I planned to do. Ted pointed out the pass to the next valley. It was a hard hike for me. I was out of shape, soft from a summer of moving and eating and not enough work.

There was snow toward the top. I was a little dizzy. We were climbing past thirteen thousand feet and the air was brittle. Once on the ridge I lost Ted and continued to follow footprints I thought were his. My knees were cold. My hands were stiff from pulling myself up over large chunks of reddish rocks. I followed the footprints across a drop-off along a narrow ledge because the route over the top of the ridge looked worse. I kept thinking that this was supposed to be an easy hike.

The ledge was narrow and my boots were slick. There was one second when I knew if I didn't put my right foot forward I would fall off. So I walked forward. On the other side, though, things were impossible. I had nowhere to go but up an overhang of slippery rocks or down the sheer jagged side of the mountain.

I figured I had followed the wrong footsteps. I lost one of my mittens. "Ted," I called out.

"Where are you?" he answered. "What are you doing down there?"

"I thought this was the trail," I yelled up.

I could see his face, but not his body. His face hung out over the ridge and above his face was the navy sky.

"I can't help you," he said. "You'll have to climb up so I can reach you from here."

I climbed far enough so Ted could put his arm over the edge and we grasped hands to wrists.

When Steve was sick I often felt like I was off the trail— one mitten lost, heart beating fast, face white, the rock and ice and spectacular blue sky above me.

For a long time I had no name for what was wrong. I wasn't sure if it was wrong in me or in Steve, or in our marriage. I thought maybe it was the place or the food we were eating or maybe just old loneliness. But all of a sudden things started to get strange. Steve watched more television. He stopped talking to my friends. He put on weight and started craving candy.

When we moved from Denver to Aspen I had a friend drive because my vision was shaky. I had the jitters all the way out of Denver into the mountains. I felt heavy and slow. In Aspen we lived in a large room in the basement of a friend's house. We had no kitchen, so we ate out a lot. We argued. I hated Aspen. We walked down the streets past men and women who were oiled to perfection. I screeched at Steve as we drove through town and people turned to watch as we passed. Steve told me to shut up, just shut up.

By the time we moved to the house in Little Elk Creek, Steve was having trouble at his job. But I didn't know that. We thought we would be living in the valley for at least two years. I had just unpacked boxes of presents from our wedding a year before. I traveled to New England to pick up a car my parents had given us.

I was still with my family over Labor Day, in Vermont, in the house where I spent weekends growing up. Steve called and told me he had been fired. I thought he was joking. He wasn't. All that night I knew that something horrible would happen.

Steve flew East and we drove the car back to Colorado. We spent the early fall trying to figure out what to do. We had no savings. We were renting an expensive house. A friend offered Steve a job in Massachusetts at a new magazine, and we decided to move as soon as we could. Sometimes Steve was not anyone I recognized as he hammered nails into the big wooden boxes we used to ship our dishes, books, towels, and pans to western Massachusetts. We cheered ourselves thinking we would be closer to my parents; we were talking about having a baby.

Before we knew Steve was sick we went skiing not far from our house in Leeds, Massachusetts, a town that was just a short walk away from Steve's new office in an old mill. The snow wasn't good, it was very cold out, the ticket to ski in these woods was expensive, and I was tired. I picked up a map at the warming hut and plotted our way around the touring center. I hadn't counted on some of the trails being closed or the snow being too deep or too rotten to plow through.

Steve was having a difficult time. He couldn't seem to remember how to move his legs. To go back would have been just as far as finishing the route, so we went ahead. It got dark. Steve could no longer lift his knees to push the skis ahead. I took my skis off but he refused to take his off. I started screaming at him. I didn't know what to do. I was as cold as I'd ever remembered being. I was afraid we would both get hypothermia. People passed us and looked at me as if I were crazy, screaming at my husband to take his skis off and walk. Finally Steve took the skis off and we walked the final mile to the car.

On the way home a strut came loose and Steve had to tie it up with some rope we found in the car. We didn't talk to each other the whole way home through the dark. Once we got there Steve took a long shower. When he came out he couldn't remember what we had done that day.

A YEAR AGO, shortly after Steve died, I had a hard time seeing things for what they were. I saw electricity in each movement. I couldn't look at bare skin; it burned me. I had a hard time sitting next to my sister in the car. I kept getting stuck on the movement of her arm to the steering wheel. It seemed like the most dangerous arm in the world. I was prey to everyone. For days the eyes of one of my students haunted me.

I decided to concentrate on birds. The variations in their feathers, the way they held the sunflower seeds in their beaks or knocked the seed against a branch. The way they fought for position on the feeder.

I wanted to fall apart but my body kept feeding itself, kept getting up in the morning, kept filling the bird feeder, kept stuffing the logs into the stove.

IN THIS WIDE OPEN COUNTRY I've been sitting on the porch reading about elk as the elk feed south of here on the refuge. On my morning run I pass rabbit brush. The elk eat the low, thorny bushes, sometimes browsing too close and getting sharp bits of twig or burrs in their mouths. This occasionally causes a disease called *necrotic stomatitis* and eventually death.

The elk, according to Olas Murie, who studied them around Jackson Hole for many years, usually eat grasses. He writes in *The Elk of North America*:

> *Elk prefer grass ranges, especially in winter, and grass is often the dominant item in the diet at any time of the year when it is sufficiently available, although naturally in certain environments, especially when the grass has been grazed down or snow-covered, other types of forage will be the chief food.*

Often, he writes, they bed down in a patch of reedgrass or sedge without using it for food. Elk have been known to attack a dog who menaces a calf, and weak calves have been attacked by eagles. Elk bugle and snort and paw but are, for the most part, quiet animals.

I go out on the elk refuge in a sleigh. The driver is a woman who looks like she belongs in a painting by Winslow Homer. She tells me when to stand and when to sit. I am the only passenger on a sleigh that can hold thirty. We talk about moose and then, as we draw closer to the cluster of bulls, about elk. There is no sound except the quiet breathing of the horses pulling us across the grasslands.

She points out a short-eared owl. "They have all sorts of methods of cooperation set up," she says.

I hear a squeaking noise and ask, "What's that?"

The driver says, "That's elk. Some people think it's a bird they can't see, but it's elk, they make all kinds of noises. It amazes me how smart the elk are and how you're always surprised when they do something they've never done before."

To our left are about a thousand elk cows and calves, a safe distance from the bulls who will cheat them out of prime feed if they stay too close. My guide points out a bull missing a leg. "It's his third year here," she says, and then she points out another who has fantastic knobs on his antlers. "They grow back the same way; I suppose it's genetic."

We circle the herd slowly, and the bitter wind blows and flattens the soft colors of the winter land. We move in browns and whites against a pale sky. The elk stand out against the buttes to the east. They are pawing through the snow to get at the grass grown rich through the long summer days. Or chewing their cud as we watch. Some rear up for a minute in a mock clash, but nothing happens.

"They're really in good shape for this time of year," she says, "we've had such light cover."

We are the only people in this valley and the elk herds stretch out in dark clusters as far as we can see.

THE SNOW IS COMING down again this morning. I walked out yesterday during a break when all the sky cleared for sunset, except the bank of purple clouds stuck on the Tetons. The memory of the land that stretches all around me makes the enclosure of these days bearable. If I could reach far enough, I could pull the top off this storm and see clear across the flat, high plains again. I still have power up my sleeve.

I counted ten moose on my way back from skiing yesterday. Dark brown and lumpy, they position themselves on the sage lands or in the river bottoms. Earlier, I watched one who appeared old, I'm not sure why. He was very large and not as dark as the others and he watched me as I watched him. Then he figured I was safe and started pawing the earth along the river where there was willow brush to browse.

He would lift his slender leg up with his large and heavy foot and use it like a shovel to paw the snow away from his breakfast. He let it swing out and then hit the ground like a pendulum. I looked for him a couple of hours later and he was still in the same place but sitting, chewing peacefully.

Concentrating on moose, I forget what I'm doing. There is no car, no house, no job; there is no history. Only the moose in all his brown perfection.

LIKE A RAVEN, I watch the movements of my neighbors. Gary works today so he wears a dark blue pea coat instead of his usual telemarking gear.

Even in Kelly there are social classes. The yurt dwellers, Gary tells me, never get along with Danny Budge, the man who once plowed me out with his big truck. The town pays him to keep the roads clear in Kelly and it took me three days to get him to plow out the area in front of Ted's house.

"Danny and Linda," Gary claims, "don't approve of West Kelly."

The Budges own a substantial establishment at the end of the road. I pass it every day on my way to the post office. A large log barn, several furry cows who were chasing each other in the snow the other day, a few sturdy horses, a log house, creamy and new, and another structure, half built, to house the dump truck with the plow.

I have dinner one night with Gary in his home. I walk across the slick path from Ted's trailer. Gary lifts the latch on the wooden door and I enter the low canvas yurt. Once I'm inside he sweeps the snow from my boots with a brush and metal dustpan, throws it outside. We eat hamburgers and watch *Superman* on his television.

Already Gary and I have a history. Where does the history go between two people when one of them dies? All that landscape is lost. And for a long time after the person you loved is gone you want to tell their story, so the story you had together isn't lost. If it's an ordinary story, one by one the people you try to tell it to will stop listening. Sometimes you want to believe stories even if they aren't true.

I know most of Gary's history and he knows nothing about me. His life centers on the here and now. He makes enough money to buy food and pay the sixty-five dollar rent on his yurt space. The first year he moved here from Ohio he lived in a tent cabin.

I have a long broken history with a man who wants me to come to Norway this spring. Harald called me not long ago and I told him I would visit him in March. I met him when I was twenty-two. I worked on his family's farm. After Steve's death, I wrote him a letter.

He came to visit in the fall and now I study the large map of the world Ted has pinned to the wall. America is tiny compared to the great lumps of Asia and Africa. I find Båteng, where Harald lives, on the map and think that perhaps I could live there after all. Nowhere seems very far from anywhere else flattened and hung that way on the wall. I touch the place with my finger.

THIS MORNING LEE DONALDSON tells me that you never see moose when you're looking for them but I proved him wrong. "They do, yes, lay down in the sage," he said. "We counted thirty one day on the road to the Science School."

Ted tells me when he calls that I couldn't have seen a bull with a mother and her calf. "The bulls just don't hang around."

I saw an eagle yesterday sitting like a raven in a cottonwood full of ravens. I had to look hard to make sure it was really an eagle. Here the ravens are my favorite birds. Glossy and proud they take their scavenging seriously and do everything with bravado. They are huge birds, almost as large as the eagles that sometimes share their perch along the Kelly road above the bend in the Gros Ventre River.

These western birds are matter-of-fact in their beauty. They take everything in stride. The guidebook tells me that they're called common ravens (*Corvus corax*) but are common only in the far north and in the west, especially near heavy timber. The raven is considered our largest songbird and the call is a "low hoarse croak." They are fond of open country.

About an hour ago I could still see the bottom edge of Blacktail Butte; now the clouds have snapped themselves down like canvas, securing themselves to the plains. The snow hugs down on my woodpile, on the shoot of wheatgrass, on the edge of the log outhouse at the back of the trailer, on the top posts of angled fences. The crows are off somewhere else. No one moves in Kelly.

Soon I'll go home to Massachusetts, turn the key in the door, and enter the small cottage where I live. I never have enough light in the downstairs room and upstairs the loft burns with light at noon.

NO ONE, at least not the Saturday postmistress's husband, believes that this calm will last. I shovel out the car, collect the mail, and decide to put the woodpile to rights today. The landscape is filled in now and different after snow, the pockets between the sagebrush soft, everything brilliant instead of glowing with those burnished colors of early winter.

I am different after snow. After these days of snow and wind. Washed thin by thinking and not thinking, by dreaming and not dreaming, by watching the flakes of snow collect on the edge of log buildings outside the window.

After skiing yesterday, I swam like a tropical fish in a large heated pool, my body liquid, my hair freezing in the falling snow, pulling my way like a waterbug across the warm surface of the pool.

The body heals itself in time. I have pulled the pieces

back into myself and polished them and fit them back together. I can almost run without thinking of anything except
the tiny perfect tracks of mule deer marking the road, or the
squirrel chittering high in the pine, or the sweep of yellow
brush, red-brown brush above the snow-covered pasture, or
the river sliding coldly past, or the flock of wintering water-
birds I startle each time I run across the bridge near the
Teton Valley Ranch sign.

Light snow this morning, long sleep last night, body
breathing, head clearing, sun due in the afternoon.

2

Possibly there is greater palatability in the very newest
vegetation—difficult for man to measure but detected by the
elk—that lures animals upward in the wake of the retreating
snow; or perhaps there is a stimulant in the early spring
atmosphere that creates an impulse to travel—and travel would
naturally be over accustomed routes; or maybe there is actual
nostalgia for remembered summer pastures.
OLAS MURIE, *The Elk of North America*

It is late March and I am flying to Alta, Norway. The woman sitting next to me is a talk show host in Oslo. She has a red bandanna tied around her throat. The plane traces a route across a map in my mind that matches the map hanging in Ted's house. Harald wants to marry me. He wants a child.

The plane dips low. I can almost touch the edge of the earth where it hits the Arctic Ocean and disappears. It is my second visit to Båteng, a village on the Tana River at the far northern corner of Norway. In a few weeks on April 9th, it will be two years since Steve's death.

WHEN I FIRST WENT to Båteng, I was very young. It was a year after I graduated from college. I took the mail boat up the coast and stopped at the Lofoten Islands. A woman I met on the town pier invited me to stay at her home in town.

"In the north country," she said, "people are still good to each other." She took me in, she told me, because I looked much younger than I was. I was carrying a large pack, off to work on a farm in the far north for several months. When I woke in the morning, she showed me a plant that had just flowered that night. The bloom was fluted and red. It was, she told me, the first time the plant had bloomed in ten years.

On the boat again I stood on the lower deck and watched the sun on the water at midnight with two men who nodded and smoked as they talked. We were far enough north that the sun doesn't set in the summer, and the winters are dark. A woman from Long Island taking the ferry to the North Cape said, "You wanted to get away from everything."

I said, "No."

"Couldn't you do this sort of thing in the States?" she asked.

I saw a herd of reindeer swimming across the harbor at Harstad and watched as the landscape flattened and grew long and dark at the edges.

In Båteng, I lived in a house with a farmer and his wife and two of their three sons. The middle son lived with his wife and two children in the basement of the house. My room upstairs was narrow with a tiny window. The farm was a cluster of buildings—a barn; a split-level house painted lime green; the original house, tall and narrow, now an office for a Mazda dealership; and a red sauna shed with one round window. The family farmed fields by the river and on the edge of the forest. The fields were bare and cold in May, snow in patches on the low hills across the Tana River in

Finland. My favorite places on the farm were the sauna and the dairy.

I liked the way the calves bit at my arms and licked my shoulders with their rough tongues. I got used to the smell of cow dung as I shoveled it clear of the stalls. I walked up to the forest where the birch trees were leafing out. When I ran above the town on the paved road, I could almost feel the earth turn.

One night I walked south along the village road, past woven rugs on a clothesline and lambs and cows in the small fields. The light had that special northern clarity. I felt all the bare cold that comes up from the earth and above me all the bare clouds—purple and gray. A stack of wood seemed as light as a sponge.

As the days grew warmer I began to like my life in Båteng more and more. I knew something was happening to me.

After a month of working on the farm, I fell in love with Harald, a bachelor and the eldest son, ten years older than I was.

He managed the farm and owned the Mazda dealership with his two brothers. Harald could speak several languages. He knew where to find the bird he called the English eagle and showed me where foxes lived in a sandy esker near the village. He was a sportsman, he told me, and proved it in long walks across the *vidda* and, many years later, in his skill at skiing. I was twenty-two and in a strange and beautiful place. Harald was powerful and mysterious. I was afraid of him at first.

We picked cloudberries in the forest, sweet salmon-colored berries, and ate them with fresh cream and sugar. I swam in the Tana, a river that flows to the Arctic Ocean but warms quickly, its shallow, clear water thick with salmon as large as small children. I started to learn a few words of Lappish, or Samisk, the language of most of the people along the river.

We walked hours into the forest to waterfalls lit at night with the low sun of the north. The light glowed under the birch leaves and illuminated the tiny red spores of moss. After days of work in the barn and the fields, we took saunas in the little shed. I shook the sweet branches dipped in cold water on my body, soft in the steam from the heated rocks.

One early morning Harald's father touched my breast as we sat together drinking coffee before we went to the barn.

"This wasn't something he should have done," Astrid, Harald's sister-in-law assured me.

I went off to the forest and slept out in a clearing near a reindeer herder's hut. Harald and I had spent a couple of nights there before, but now I couldn't find the key. On my way out of the village, I had passed Harald's father who was hammering a reindeer skin to the barn to dry. I was afraid and angry. Harald told me later his mother was sure I'd been eaten by a bear.

When the weather was clear, I pulled cut hay to dry over wires strung across the fields. We ate pieces of salmon grilled over a fire of sticks gathered on the river bank, where slim black boats were tethered. In the evening I would hear Harald walking across the gravel of the road, a white pitcher in his hand, to collect milk from the dairy for dinner.

After a party one night when people were dancing near

a blazing fire near the river, Harald told me his uncle had said to him, "You will lose the American girl."

"You see," Harald said, "I don't know what it is—this word 'love.' I feel for you a little more, not less."

One morning I got up and fainted onto the kitchen floor. I cut my head, and Harald's younger brother Knut, who was visiting from Bergen, patched up the gash. Later, Harald took me to the clinic several miles away and I was stitched and bandaged.

I looked at my face in the mirror in the bathroom and asked, who am I? What's happened? I wondered if I still had a soul.

We hiked up a mountain not far from Båteng called Rasttigaisa with Axel, a student from Germany who was also working on the farm. I had a hard time keeping up with Harald on the long walk to the top.

"You can if you will, Sharon," he told me as I struggled across the rocky ground. I remembered that statement off and on as I struggled across other uneven landscapes in my life.

My parents called. Their voices sounded like people I knew from another life. They demanded I meet my grandmother in England. We had planned a trip together before I left for Norway.

I told Harald I was leaving soon. It was early September and already the birches had turned their brittle gold. In a few weeks, the reindeer owners would herd the reindeer into pens to notch the ears of the calves with marks of ownership. On one long walk over the humps of moss and tiny bushes of the forest, I was so cold I couldn't move my hands. I couldn't see more than a foot ahead in the mist. We slept by a waterfall thundering into the night.

I imagined that I would return. I could see myself living in a house above the town.

When I got home later that fall I knew something was wrong with me. I thought it was a broken heart. My doctor performed several tests. He told me I had a parasite from eating raw fish. I wrote to Harald. He sent me a silk shawl and photographs of the new shop he was building.

"When will you come to visit us in Båteng?" he asked in his short letter.

I was not convinced that he loved me.

NOW, I WAKE on my first morning in a new cottage Knut has built on the edge of a small field near his parents' house. Black, shiny crows skim the white field. Harald takes a sauna as the fire spits in the stove. I admire the practical beauty of the cottage: sleeping closet in the kitchen, the boards of the walls washed with white paint, rag rugs scattered on the floors. The porch faces the Tana River. I can see the barn where I used to work and Harald's uncle's house, blue and peeling in the birch woods to my left.

I want to learn more about the *joik*, a traditional song. I've read that the missionaries who came to this area in the early seventeenth century didn't approve of joiking. The songs were connected to a shamanistic religion. Even now, Harald points out rocks known to be sacred when we ski in the forest.

Harald and I ski up the slope above the village to where

Lief Wigelius lives. He's a composer and a singer. The joik, he tells me, started around the fire at the beginning of time and was sung to soothe the reindeer. And he sings a version of what it may have sounded like—"Oulu, oulu, oulu."

"I am right now beginning to make a joik about you, Sharon," he says, "a slow song to show how you skied up the hill after Harald."

"When I was a boy—eight years old," he tells me, "I had to speak Norwegian in school—they made you. And I only knew on that first day two words *pole* and *bil*—car—because I asked on the way there."

I'm comfortable sitting in Lief's house above Båteng, the lighted ski track below us in the dusk. Lief leans toward us as he talks. Harald flips through a scrapbook detailing Lief's years as a champion cross-country skier.

"If you knew a man and wanted to make a song about him or a place or a woman you missed, you would think about them and make the melody like them, slow or fast or peaceful, and then the words would come. Joiks weren't only about reindeer. I think our songs, the joiks, are a lot like Willie Nelson or Johnny Cash songs. They come from the same kind of country—reindeer, cattle."

He tells me he sings "These Old Cotton Fields" in Samisk to soothe his two-year-old to sleep.

Lief's wife, Harald tells me later, beats him. He drinks too much.

ONE AFTERNOON Harald's mother, Ellen Merethe, comes to the door of the cottage which I've left open while I write, the low sun of March hitting the soft colors of the rugs and wood. I motion for her to come in, and we sit at the table in the kitchen and talk in our own fashion, pointing to words in the dictionary, tracing our fingers on the maps of Norway and the United States. "Will you eat meat?" she asks me. "Will you come back in the summer?"

Some days the early dark of March, the stretch of the low landscape all around me, the snap of cold and night that comes down when I'm alone by the fire waiting for Harald to finish work scare me. I can't see any way out of the horizon. I call my mother in a panic. All I can feel is the whiteness of those hills, the gray edge of the water, the smooth stones of the Arctic beaches. So smooth sometimes I think I, too, would like to be ground like that by waves and then put to rest on some gritty beach.

ONE DAY WE WATCH Harald's father stuff a paper sack full of candy in his pocket for the ride on a snowmobile to Eldor's hut. He is cutting a trail for us, dragging a pack wrapped in skin on the back of a track setter. We catch up to him later, lost in the forest and then lost when the reindeer herders' snowmobile tracks veer off left and right across the low hills.

"That hill, there, that black hill," Harald tells me, "at the bottom is Eldor's dirt hut." His geography is printed, a lineage of words impressed against the white I see all around.

We ski up to the forest, to a hut we walked to together twelve years ago. I saw Eldor's hut from the outside then, a small round building made out of rough wood with a sod roof. Through a square window the size of my face, I could see wooden benches built into the walls for beds and a tiny wooden table pressed under the window.

It's a long ski through the pink-tipped landscape, the cold fingers of the sun—just back from three months of darkness in early February—now present for a good part of the day. We pass a place where there are buzzards' nests, and Harald told me a long time ago about boys throwing the eggs off the cliff.

"Did you do it too, when you were thirteen?" I ask.

"Yes, of course," he answers.

When we stop for lunch, sitting on stones just off the track, Harald tells me more about the joiks, or *juoi'gat* in Lappish. The joik was a kind of cooperation between the people guarding the reindeer and the wolves. The wolves didn't attack the reindeer herd because they heard people, and the reindeer were comforted by the songs.

We don't eat the dried reindeer meat and smoked salmon we ate when we first took this path together. This time it's cheese and bread. When I was here before our meals were a combination of climate and tradition. In the house in Båteng the main meal was served at two. Often something ladled out of a pot and sopped up with coarse, delicious bread I learned to make. We served eleven workmen at lunch. Reindeer meat and potatoes were the center of the meal, the meat sometimes seared, sometimes boiled with carrots. The marrow was the favorite part.

Harald and his father would crack the larger bones on the floor with a wooden block and a hammer. His father cracked the smaller bones with his knuckles, polished hard like wood. If we tired of reindeer, there was always salmon, caught fresh that day, hauled up in nets and clubbed on the edge of the long, narrow black boat. We simmered the salmon in a soup of potatoes, onions, shiny salmon eyes, sil-ver skin.

When we were haymaking we would break at two for our meal: thick slices of bread covered with jam and butter, salmon cooked on sticks over the fire I had coaxed into a cooking fire. For hikes we would pack a knapsack full of salted salmon and half-cooked reindeer meat, bread, butter, a teapot. If we were lucky we found bitter little blueberries and caught mountain trout, fiery slim fish we gutted on the edge of the rocky tarns. We threw the eggs on the moss and cloudberries for the foxes and buzzards to eat.

Other details have changed in the north since my first visit there. The ski track lit all through the long winter is new. I notice more cars on the roads. Nothing seems as re-mote or protected as it did. Astrid and Terje have a house on the hill behind the farm. When I was last here, they lived in the same house as Harald and his parents, waiting for per-mission to build on farmland.

Knut, Harald's youngest brother, a doctor, has started a clinic in Karasjok where he and his wife, also a doctor, work. Their clinic specializes in diseases peculiar to the north and to Sami people. When I tell Knut about the parasite I got from, according to my doctors, eating raw salted salmon the last time I was in Norway, he asks to have the records sent from the hospital in Connecticut.

When we visit Knut and Siev in Karasjok, I'm surprised by the size of the town, all the new houses on the hills above the river.

"To Knut," Siev tells me, "Båteng is almost heaven on

earth. But before we had our house, Knut would leave me with the children and Harald's mother and go off to the sauna and fishing with the Solbakks or others and I would be left."

Harald's father is much older, and I know that he's been very sick. One day he comes out of the house with two willow grouse and holds them up to show us as we wax our skis. The bodies are white with one black spot.

"We'll have these on Sunday," he says in Norwegian and I smile. He's told me that the pieces of plastic cut from shopping bags on the willow grouse traps are to scare away foxes and buzzards, to keep them from stealing the catch.

WE VISIT ASTRID and her children while Terje works in the new shop the three brothers have opened up in Tana Bru, the nearest town north on the river. We've been to Tana Bru to the shop. Harald's brother Terje nods when I say hello. It's as if I'm erased from the present and the past all at once.

"Yes," Harald answers when I ask, "he is like this sometimes, he is often like this."

"He can't be a great salesman," I say.

Harald says, "Yes, Knut says so too."

"If you are welcome," Harald tells me later as we stand on the doorstep of Astrid's house, "they will offer you coffee."

We enter the house and Harald's nephew greets us, "Kan du Samisk?" he asks.

"No," I answer.

We move into the living room overlooking the Tana, dark now and cold. Merethe, a baby when I was last here, comes in, and then Astrid with cups and coffee and little cakes. Merethe, Harald tells me later, wants to be a writer.

"See, you are welcome," Harald says.

The coffee is very hot and the cakes sweet. Merethe opens an album of pictures on my lap and there I am, twelve years before, holding her up to the camera, a round, laughing baby.

WE SKI TO THE CLEARING where the hut sits beside a lake. I unsnap my skis and stoop to enter. Harald throws our gear onto the wooden benches. I watch him start a fire in the little stove, still warm from someone else. Soon Harald's asleep and I'm propped on my elbow watching the mild northern sun fall through the short birches printed with a black growth. We're on the edge of a frozen lake full of char, covered with snow and prints of reindeer, the tracks of a wolf who calls out at dusk.

I examine the hut, the split birch logs, paper, plastic and then sod—thatch for the roof. Some insulation is stuffed around the door frame. Men who hunt willow grouse in the birch thickets and fish in the lakes that surround us sleep here sometimes. I rub my fingers on the worn bench.

This type of shelter was used by Sami people, Harald tells me, until about 1954 or so, as a home. The wealthier people started building timber houses of split logs around that same time but the poorer ones lived in huts.

THE NEXT DAY we ski up to the edge of the treeless vidda. The land goes off in rolling swells across the top of the earth.

We see the marks of many reindeer and foxes and scare up a couple of willow grouse (the eagle eats their white bodies clean) and hare. Back at Eldor's hut there is no past or future. One tiny window faces the yard where Harald splits wood. Sunset glows in pinks and blues on the landscape. An eagle calls in a high keening note. Harald knocks the ax through the slim birch logs for the little stove. I can hear the trickle of water under the waterfall where we saw an eagle's nest littered with the feathers of willow grouse. Suddenly poems I wrote about this place years ago come alive, a net across time.

I try to see myself living in the forest above Båteng. Can I live with Harald, I wonder, and then I remember that I don't really fit in anywhere with much conviction anymore. Steve's death has set me loose from any landscape I know.

I dream over and over that Steve is still alive. In one dream we're driving in a van after I've found Steve wandering streets again. He has a long face, unshaven, and long hair, and later he talks in another language. We travel to a place where there are huge red stone buildings and I say, this is the French-Canadian way of building. And then Steve gets out of the van and tries to run. He falls and his heart is beating so hard I'm afraid it will break and his left arm is weak and I'm trying to hold him up on the snow and I can't. I keep trying to find someone who will help us get to the hospital. I wake myself crying for help.

On our ski back to Båteng we come to an area pounded down by snowmobiles. Harald teaches me how to skate, and I fly across the packed snow, my arms pulling hard against the poles.

MY TRIP TO FINNMARK seems to finish something started twelve years before, breaks a spell. I make a list of the attributes of the child we might have. I think about commuting between this world and the other.

After a week in Båteng, Harald drives me to the airport in Lakselv.

"You have a problem," he says.

"Which one?" I ask.

"About living in Båteng."

I take the mail plane out of Lakselv and fly south. The plane is just large enough for several orange mail sacks, two pilots, and two passengers.

"We will fly low," one of the pilots tells me. Below me there are glaciers, and reindeer running, half-buried in wind-blown snow.

I have desired to go
Where springs not fail,
To fields where flies no sharp and sided hail
And a few lilies blow.

And I have asked to be
Where no storms come,
Where the green swell is in the havens dumb,
And out of the swing of the sea.
GERARD MANLEY HOPKINS

The walnuts are falling on the roof as I write. They litter the grass with their hard green skins. The squirrels are running up and down the trunks of the black walnuts and turning the nuts over and over again in their paws. I watch them gnaw the nut clean or bury it in the garden.

It is September and I am once again in the cottage in Massachusetts. Although I have a post office box, mail comes sometimes addressed to me at Grove Hill, the old name for this place.

Yesterday I spent the early afternoon reading about widows and death. And then I went running. It doesn't help to read that I'm a statistic, my emotions are predictable, grief is a psychological state. That feeling crazy is normal. That often widows are afraid of going out of control. That the images of strangers that pop up like splinters are all normal. I am not going crazy. My eyes are still in the correct position on my face. Apples are falling from trees. Months are going by.

I ran along the river never shaking the sense that I was being followed. I passed a truck parked by the side of the road on my route back and was convinced someone would hop out and attack me. Later, I saw two men fishing and figured it was their truck.

I won't use cans or open boxes. All the widows I read about have children. I wonder if somehow these words will give me back myself. There's a ridge across my big toenails just halfway up the nail. I wonder if this is when Steve died and how long it takes for nails to grow out.

I DIDN'T RETURN to Båteng in the summer. In June, a month before the haymaking season, Harald came to visit me, and then I went to Colorado and spent the summer there. I made a bargain with my employer. The college would give me a permanent job if I would finish my doctorate, which I had begun at the University of Denver years earlier. I lived with a friend in a new townhouse and planted a miniature garden in his tiny backyard. As I rode my bike to the university, I thought I saw Steve walking to the printer's shop across the park. I imagined him petting his cat or leaning over a line of type. I tried to concentrate on books and papers and raising my hand in class.

HARALD TOLD ME A STORY many years ago. It was about a little girl called Merethe. Once, he said, on a long migration across the highlands, a child fell off a reindeer and slept in the snow. In the morning the child woke up and started crying. All the family and the reindeer were way ahead of the little girl and she was lost. She pulled at her nose and sang a song as loud as she could about the bear. Maybe the bear will come, she thought, and I'll go to sleep in her fur.

There was a small light in the sky and the child wondered how much longer until the sun. She was smart. She brushed off her tunic and pulled her blue cap down to her eyes and laced up her boots. Snow had fallen all night so there were no tracks to follow. But she set off in the same direction as the gray in the black world.

I'll find someone, she thought.

She was a sturdy little girl. She walked for a long time and passed little birches and, once, a tiny pine. There were no animals. There were no birds. She saw some smoke.

She followed it to a group of stones. There was a crack in one of the rocks like a mouth, and she pushed her body through to a room lined with skins. Oh.

"Tell me where mother and father are."

An old woman sat in the center of the room. "Sit down, Merethe, and let me see your feet."

She took the child's feet in her hands and rubbed them until they stung and spat with heat.

"There. Your people are a long way from here. You must walk away from the light into the darkest place in the sky, then you will find them."

The woman gave Merethe a sledge and a reindeer and some milk and cheese pressed and wrapped in moss. The child set off across the vidda again.

She traveled for so long that one day the sun came out.

She came to a lake near a grove of old birch. There was a man, a big man, cutting fish from a net. The fish were spotted with pink and yellow. Merethe watched the man split the fish with a thick knife and rip out the guts and the tiny eggs in the female. The eggs glowed on the moss like red fox eyes, and the water in the little lake grew still as night in midwinter.

Merethe knew where she was. She walked down the hill from the little tarn and saw her mother and father camped with the reindeer on a flat place near the Tana.

But when she put her arms around her mother's neck, her mother said, "Go away Merethe. You come into my heart too many times. You are as white and hard as the reindeer bones on the high fell near Rasttigaisa. If I went there I would not know the difference."

I have been going back across my past as if it were a landscape. Each time I come to a place where the mother and father should be camped, where the mother and father will recognize me, it is always the same. I don't live there anymore and I have been dead a long time. Look, my bones are fossils on the bottom of the ancient lake. And the past will not lead me to myself or to Steve.

Harald called me last night and told me the seals were eating the salmon.

"John Tregge," he said, "has found a new woman, twenty-two years old. Odivar is still missing."

He was cheerful. He had found an injured eagle in the forest and nursed it back to health.

"You're getting old," he told me. "Soon, you won't be able to have a child."

TODAY I'M GRADING student essays. I underline and make notes and pile the papers on the floor. I have no time to think, hardly any time to mourn. There are stacks of books all over the house. When I'm not teaching, I study eighteenth century English literature. I learn that Alexander Pope liked to garden. He had grottos filled with falling water.

I think about the great blue heron I see in the morning at the pond below the VA Hospital. She stands at the edge, fishing in the mist, her long neck darting in and out. Once, I watched a heron somewhere else standing still for a long time. His eye was rimmed with black, the long feathers of his mating plumage lifted in the slight breeze.

The heron has fished the shallow pond each fall since I moved here. Perhaps there is a reason for the repetition of place. She seems to like to visit this narrow pond by the busy road each time she flies south. She stays a week or so and then moves on. But she doesn't expect much—just a place to rest and eat, a familiar temporary habitat on her long journey down the coast.

4

By nature trees do rot when they are grown,
And plums and apples thoroughly ripe do fall,
And corn and grass are in their season mown,
And time brings down what is both strong and tall.
But plants new set to be eradicate,
And buds new blown to have so short a date,
Is by His hand alone that guides nature and fate.

ANNE BRADSTREET

My office at the college where I work in Springfield, Massachusetts, not far from Leeds, looks out at a parking lot. It is the end of February and the tree just outside my window still holds the tightly folded buds of the season.

Basketball was invented at this college. Every year at least one student writes a paper about basketball. The first baskets, I learn from each of these papers, were peach baskets. Until a few years ago the Basketball Hall of Fame was in a building on the edge of the campus.

We hire people who like to play sports, who relate to the students. I have to think hard to come up with good sports metaphors for my classes. The best I can do is to talk about skiing.

Often, my classes are filled with students in sweat suits.

The campus winds along a lake called Lake Massasoit,

but students tell me it's called Mill Pond on the maps they've looked at. It's polluted, they tell me, from lawn fertilizer and dog droppings.

"Really?" I ask.

"Yes," a student assures me. "You can eat one fish a year caught from the lake and that's it. They stock it you know."

The lake is slate blue now and cold. The greasy surface reflects the gray sky and fish winter under the surface. Soon, it will snow.

This morning I got up in the dark to run down the hill to meet a friend in the park. I am afraid of the dark hill. I wonder when spring will come. I watch the silhouettes of maples against the yellow street lights that don't throw much light.

A tiny sliver of a moon glows on the edge of the sky. We run around the park and watch as the wintering geese sleep in the pond. We pass the same people every morning as we run.

I'm warm by the time I run back up the hill. By then I can hear the pileated woodpecker calling out, and sometimes in the fall or early spring when they come through, a hawk will be preening in the highest branches of the tall pines near my house.

AT FIRST I'm not sure what's happening. Cisco is yelling. Chris is holding himself back. I forget I'm in a classroom. It is 10:15 on the large face of the clock on the green wall. Daniel sits across from me and shakes his head. He looks more engaged than I've ever seen him. Everyone else is looking at me and then at Cisco and Chris. I wonder if this is what the start of a murder looks like.

Cisco says, "You can't call me a flash dancer!"

And Chris yells back, "Hey man, you can't tell me I'm smokin' a doobie!"

Cisco breaks away and heads for the door and the class urges him back. He pivots there and heads back across the room to sit next to Chris, their backs almost touching.

Cisco and I have violent fights about sentence fragments. He sees me as a tyrant sometimes, slashing and burning his papers. We have long discussions about standards and different types of written language. The class usually listens silently to these discussions.

"You want to take away my creativity," he yells, "my individuality!"

Today in class, after listening to most of the students read their essays, Cisco said, "It's like being in a wood at dusk and slowly you start to see the trees—I'm starting to see the faces in this class like that."

One day when I was listening to Cisco my heart started to beat faster and faster. I was sitting in the tiny windowless Writing Center in the library, my back against the brick wall facing Cisco across the desk. I had been drinking a very large cup of coffee. Soon I couldn't breathe. After Cisco left I called my doctor's office in Connecticut. I described the symptoms.

"You better get to a hospital as fast as you can," his nurse said.

I had ridden to work with a colleague, so I walked over to the building where we teach and had her called out of a class. At the hospital they hooked me up to machines and measured my heart. After a while the doctor spoke to me.

"Your heart is fine," she said. "It looks like a reaction to caffeine. I'd stay away from it."

But my heart isn't fine, I want to tell her. It's not the right size or beating at the right rate. Sometimes I feel as if I have no heart. Like the pigeons I used to see, their hearts snapped out by the sharp teeth of my neighbor's cats in Denver.

CISCO'S LAST PROJECT for the term is to write a letter to the dean and the head of the physical education department. He's been teaching aerobics on campus all semester to classes of up to one hundred students, three times a week. I went to one of the classes. He performed with power and confidence. The school has refused to pay Cisco for these classes.

Things happen to Cisco all the time. He was hit by a car about a week ago when he was jogging. He loses computer disks with papers on them and bags full of books and homework. He's trying to decide whether to give up and drop out, or go back to Germany, perhaps, and teach aerobics there.

"You put your hand out to me," he said a while ago, "but when I look for you, you're not there." Often an hour or two late for appointments, he sometimes shows up on the wrong day.

"I have been here for you," I said the other day. And he said, "Yes, you have been."

"You shouldn't beat me up so much," I told him. And he said, "Yes, you're right."

ONCE A WEEK, a graduate student brings portions of his thesis for me to look at. He has a type of epilepsy that can interfere with his writing. He often can't remember changes we've discussed. We work and rework the same sentence over and over.

Dave is a poet, he tells me, and one day brings his work for me to see. The poems are typed and collected in a black binder notebook. I flip through his intricate, beautiful poems. I ask him to read a few for one of my classes.

In late fall he showed me a maple leaf, the largest leaf I've ever seen. "You found that here?" I asked. And he said yes.

"What will you do with it?"

"Oh, press it probably, put some calligraphy around it, and frame it. I might give it to my niece."

ON THE DRIVE HOME today my knuckles are white, I notice, as I look down at my hands on the steering wheel. I know this bend in the road by heart, but that doesn't make the drive easier. Once over the river, cold with late winter frost, the drive goes straight north.

Soon the hawks will return along the highway. I often see seven or more on my drive south. A student tells me her class studied an albino hawk who hunts near the shopping mall. I saw the hawk every night as I drove north in the fall, perched on a pole near the highway watching.

Sometimes the hawks are tattered and fierce, hanging onto their branches like bits of garbage thrown up in a storm. Often, if I'm close enough, I can see the sleek shining feathers of the red-tailed hawks, their hard talons gripping the slim branches of maples and oaks, their heads moving back and forth against the bare branches, hunting small animals in the grassy edges of the highway.

I can't stop thinking about a woman I spoke to this

morning on the phone. I called the American Cancer Society in Springfield. I wanted to find a support group for young widows. I've tried, off and on for the past couple of years, to find a group through the area hospitals or churches, but most of those listed were for people who were older.

Once I went to a meeting advertised in the paper as "Help for Young Widows and Widowers." It was in the basement of a church. We sat on metal chairs in a circle and told our stories. A man and several women in the group had been meeting for a few weeks. They had children and complained about the problems of being a single parent. I was embarrassed to confess I had no children. It seemed to mark me as not one of them. I did not go to the next meeting. One day I saw the man ordering meat in the grocery store and I turned the corner away from him.

I think often about the suspension of my life. I don't like the idea that I want to be rescued. The leader of the group was married again and seemed quite happy. Her husband had died a year before. I often feel like a misfit, carrying the story of Steve's death around like another limb.

I listened, this morning, to a woman whose husband died about the same time as Steve: three years ago in April. She told me all about the trouble she's been having and how she still feels married.

"Nobody ever calls," she said, "because they know I'm not married and everybody's a couple.

"When he first died, I called all over the place, and tried to find some widow's groups, but they were all old widows, over sixty or so, and I have no one to talk to. All I did was drink that first year. I'd come home and drink myself to sleep.

"My husband," she said, "weighed only eighty-five pounds when he died. I knew and he knew that he was dying, but we pretended he wasn't. I took tranquilizers for the anxiety attacks. I thought it would help to work at the Cancer Society, but I have to give a film and the films are about hospitals and dying, and then I have to give presentations, and one of the kids is fifteen and he has cancer of the kidneys and he says, see you next year, but I know he won't be here next year."

And then she told me how her husband was sick for two years and they thought he was better and then he got sick again.

"Who do you have?" she asked me.

I said, "My parents."

"I don't have any parents and my kids are all gone except for the nineteen-year-old and he's never here. I think it would help having a support group. I come home and I talk to the fish and the dog and the cat and they think I'm crazy and yesterday I felt so bad I went to my neighbors'. I was crying and I said, 'Can I have a cup of tea?' and they said, 'Yes,' but they looked at me like I was crazy.

"And you know, I'm going to a psychologist and I asked her if she thought it was good that I was working here, and you know they never answer you; they just ask you another question.

"We even," she said, "had the color of the truck picked out. It was going to be blue."

When I cross the wide river, metallic in this light, it all comes to me. The flocks of wintering birds I can't make out clearly in the hazy, cold sky; the thought of snow falling in Springfield; the woman's voice on the phone; trumpets blaring as I drive fast enough but not so fast that the cops will stop me; the face of one of my students, round, red, blotched, his streak of maroon hair popping down over his forehead; Cisco yelling to me from his dorm window as I walked by the lake at noon; the gritty highway flying under the gritty wheels of the car; the smokestacks of the city flying off to the right; the Marlboro billboard looming up to the left, a cowboy smoking. And suddenly the world comes together in great broken harmony, a town I never thought I'd live near, a school where the halls smell like dirty sneakers, Steve, Steve's death, the voice of the woman on the phone and her dead husband, so small in his casket at eighty-five pounds, the past three years, the whirling birds, and all the pain of all the people flying along the highway going north, going north where I have just come from this morning.

5

The gulls began to disappear, streaming faintly like ashes
against the last fires on the sea, but still crying vastly and
collectively toward a world of distances.
JOHN HAY, *The Run*

It is spring along the Mississippi. My friend Bonnie and I are driving to Steve's grave in Monroe, Iowa. We buried him three years ago during a spring like this one, early, full of blossom. We drive the long way from her home in Rock Island west one hundred miles or so through the countryside that bends out in perfection at each dip of the road. Narrow and slippery with rain, the road goes the same way Bonnie and her husband Chris drove when they brought Steve's body back to Monroe from Iowa City for the funeral.

Chris is the director of his family's funeral home. Although he's an architect by profession, when the recession hit Portland he left the West Coast and went into business with his father. He buried Steve.

One day, after the third anniversary of Steve's death in April, I decided I was ready to visit his grave and I called Bonnie. We met years ago in Oregon in the fall when I was just out of college. She was living in an old farmhouse in a filbert orchard and wanted someone to rent a downstairs room. I answered her ad and lived in Coburg just a few months until I left for Norway when I was twenty-two.

When Steve was sick in Iowa City, Chris met me at the hospital and convinced me to stay at their apartment an hour away in Rock Island. Once there, he built a fire in the tiny fireplace and pulled a chair close to the fire for me. Their home was my refuge during the last weeks of Steve's illness and after his death.

Bonnie and I keep our fingers crossed that Axel, barely one, and Avery, just nine, will hold up for the long ride to Monroe. Avery goes to sleep. We wonder whether to wake her up for the men driving buggies filled with children wearing wide straw hats, for the lush fields full of grazing horses. Axel sleeps most of the way, too. We can't believe he's so good.

I'm bringing flowers from the gardens in Rock Island, and a rose from Chris, and Avery has her own delicate, carefully picked flowers for Steve. She was there at his funeral and remembers it.

I am afraid I won't cry when I get to the grave. I am afraid I won't be able to find it. Chris has drawn me a map. The map in my brain is distorted by vast tracts of empty space.

A friend in Denver told me a story recently about looking for her parents' graves. She had traveled a long way back to Australia where she had grown up and where her parents, who were killed in a car/train accident when she was very young, were buried. It was the first time she had gone back, the first time she had traveled the same route where the train hit the car. She was in the car, too, the only survivor of the crash.

When she got to the graveyard with her husband, she went to the office. It was an enormous place. The caretaker pointed out the location of her parents' graves on a large map. My friend and her husband looked for several hours for the graves. When they found the spot where her parents should have been buried, there was a huge hole. They were building a new chapel.

Bonnie gestures to a view of orchard, field, house, horse. The landscape of Iowa is one of the most beautiful there is. Dramatic in a painterly way, it arches and folds in various shades of green, ordered rows, the thickets of oak woods where you hunt for deer, the fat corn-fed deer, and where you beat the brush for pheasants; the perfect white frame houses surrounded by the metal pig houses or cattle in fenced fields.

Steve preferred cities. He loved the way they were lit up and sprawling. He admired the cities of the West, flat, extensive, rearing up out of prairies and plains. He always felt uneasy when he went home to Monroe, so I didn't like thinking of him there.

I had decided after many months of thinking not to visit my mother-in-law. I was afraid of what she would say. Of what we would say to each other. My last image of her, the one that stays, is when I got to the hospital in Iowa City the morning of Steve's death and she grabbed my hair as close to the roots as she could and pulled.

"I wanted more time," she said.

The doctor said, "I can't understand why it happened.

We got him out of the shower and into bed and he was fine but then everything stopped and we did a code but couldn't bring him back."

Steve's death was the last in a series of events his mother endured from his father's death in November to Steve's death a year and a half later in April. During that time Steve's brother had a stroke and the school where she worked for twenty years or more burned down.

Steve's family had welcomed me when we first met and later were engaged. I liked visiting Iowa. I would sleep late in the thick air of midsummer and run down the dirt roads past white painted farms and fields of corn and soybeans. Sometimes I'd take his father's hunting dog for a walk.

After we were married, I had a few difficult visits. I didn't like Stan, Steve's brother, and he didn't like me. He saw me as an Easterner and I objected to the way he treated Steve. Stan was his parents' favorite but it was Steve, I think, who his mother felt closest to—even though she wouldn't admit it. Steve encouraged his mother's art and her reading. He listened when she talked about what projects she was working on.

Stan had a steady job, a house, a boat, a dog, and lived only half an hour away. He liked to hunt, and when we visited in November when Steve's Dad was dying, we went out hunting pheasants. Steve's brother-in-law, Tony, shot a hen and dressed the bird in the field, threw the head over a fence. Steve told us later that there's a one hundred dollar fine for shooting a hen.

His father, Steve told me, taught them the correct way

to hunt. Neither Stan nor Steve would ever shoot a hen or carry their gun the way Tony carried his. When we went hunting with Rex, Steve's father, earlier in the year, Steve hung back with his father who was too tired to hike across the lightly frozen fields, brittle with the shorn stalks of corn, into the gullies where we tramped the bush for pheasants.

THE LAST TIME we visited Monroe we were driving east from Aspen, moving to Leeds. One night after Steve and Stan had argued, Steve went out walking alone to find some old friends, he said. He met them in a bar not far from his house. At about two or so his mother and I both woke up and met in the narrow living room. We didn't know where Steve was; we weren't sure whether we should look for him. We both knew something was wrong but didn't know how to say it.

We watched the dark street through the picture window. When we couldn't stand it any longer, we went outside in our robes and there was Steve, coming toward us huddled up in his sweatshirt against the fall air. Joyce walked back inside and left me to meet him alone.

He had gone to the golf course near the house after he left the bar and visited a memorial for his father. He sat down near the roses his mother had planted and thought about his father, he told me.

Later, Steve's mother disagreed with the way I questioned the doctors in charge of Steve's care. When I arrived at the hospital in Iowa City, the doctor in charge accused me of not taking care of Steve.

"Why wasn't he on anti-seizure medicine?" he asked.

Steve's doctor in New Haven had advised against the medication. Later the doctors in Iowa City wanted to use chemotherapy on Steve. I refused the experimental treatment after talking to the technician in charge of the project.

"Will this help Steve?" I asked.

"No," she said, "but it might help someone else."

I don't think Steve's mother approved of me driving an hour east to stay at Bonnie's home instead of in the boarding-house where she was staying.

When Steve died she was not ready for him to go. She had wanted to take care of him. He had fought pneumonia and was well enough to go home. We had been discussing a long-term care facility near Monroe. I hoped, if Steve was well enough, we could go back to Leeds. If he stayed in Iowa, I thought I might try teaching part-time at a college near where he was. I wasn't sure of anything. I moved through each hour as well as I could.

When I left the day before Steve died, he told me he loved me—he hadn't spoken in a few days except to answer yes or no. I spent those days watching Steve sleep, his breathing labored, the clouds beyond his window something natural and strange. I watched nurses adjust Steve's IV bottle, and others who left the plastic bottle of urine untouched, and another who took away a cold tray of food. One day I trimmed his beard, the strands of his hair red and black on the towel under his chin.

The man in the bed next to Steve often smiled at me. He had a black eye and his right side was paralyzed and there wasn't much chance that he would leave the hospital. "You look," he told me, "like someone I knew a long time ago."

The next morning, Steve's mother was with him. He ate breakfast with her and told one of his nurses he felt great, and then he had a seizure which he seemed to come out of and then another. Joyce called me between the two seizures, and I drove with Bonnie to the hospital, not knowing if I would see Steve before he died.

When I got there, the young nurse who walked with us around the corridors of the hospital came up to me and put her arms around me. They had been waiting for me to arrive. The door to the room was closed. When they opened the door, I saw Steve. He had strange bruises on his body and a tube down his throat. The nurse wouldn't remove the plastic tube until I told the doctor I didn't want an autopsy.

"It could help someone else," Dr. Ditwiler said.

And I said, "Just take the tube out."

I sat with Steve and held his hand.

THE LAST TIME I heard from Steve's mother she wrote that there were white chrysanthemums blooming on Steve's grave.

When we reach Monroe we drive to the graveyard two streets south of the house where Steve grew up, past the house of an old friend most people called peculiar but someone Steve found interesting, past the glue factory where another friend works, around the corner of the dirt road where I used to run when we visited Monroe, to the graveyard that had haunted me for three years.

Once, when we were visiting Steve's family, we biked over to the graveyard and stood at the entrance. Earlier, I had slammed the kitchen door at his parents' house. I felt as if I wanted to scream. I was tired of sitting at the kitchen table listening to conversations about people I didn't know, through a haze of smoke. Steve followed me outside.

"We have to get out of here," I whispered when we were in the driveway.

We got on his parents' bikes and rode around the corner past the cornfield and the golf course to the graveyard.

"You can't act this way," Steve said as we stood straddling the bikes.

I was angry and upset, crying at the entrance to the graveyard where less than two years later I would bury Steve. When I wiped my face, we took off on a tour of streets where he grew up.

Now Bonnie parks the van on the side of the graveyard where we think the grave should be. Bonnie takes Axel out of the car and changes his diaper on the rough-cut grass. Avery and I walk north through long rows of large stones looking for Steve's grave. I had forgotten there were other graves here.

I remembered an empty expanse and the place Steve was buried and two pines. The pines are there, many of them tossing in the sharp air, tossing the tips of clouds we feel we can touch.

Avery walks right up to the grave. "Here it is," she says.

"How did you know?" I ask her later.

"I don't know," she says, "I just knew."

Someone has stuck a flag in near the grave. Steve was a veteran. He was injured in a bowling alley while on duty, something we used to laugh about. Someone else has planted flowers, a couple of geraniums, a few marigolds that need to be dead-headed. We put our flowers on the small stone.

Bonnie stands near me holding Axel. I don't cry. Soon two older people walk across the gravel drive and pass us. We're playing with Axel, tossing him from one to another.

"I'm here to see my sister and brothers' graves," the woman tells us. "Where you folks from?"

The man chucks Axel under the chin.

"When we came here last," the woman, who looks about eighty, says, "I don't think there were so many. I guess they just keep dying. Who do you folks have here?" she asks me.

And I say, "My husband," but she can't hear me and she says, "Oh isn't that nice."

We walk over to the south side of the graveyard and look out across the fields of grain growing in the hot air.

"It's beautiful," Bonnie says.

I watch a hawk fly, harried by crows. He circles, the birds shaken off, his square warm body not attached to us, not attached to the earth.

6

Water is the connection. I swim clean laps in the park pool. Kicking my head back, pulling my fingers through the water that splits apart into light. My face breaks clear from the water. Bones like age pulling themselves out, the skin tightening, the lines etched, signposts.

Steve is swimming in the water with me. He's having a hard time breathing. There are many people around us. Bodies like fish glancing off my thighs and my fingertips.

A woman is swimming beside me. The loons rest easy. The lake pulls itself out around me to the pines, edge of wilderness gone tame. The woman looks right through me. I feel her body all through me as we swim.

Out on the water the boat moves slowly. The man steers the boat past the châteaux. He is speaking French. The long grassy estates come down to the water's edge. Later, a man is repairing fishnets by the fish house.

I am drinking water straight from the lake, water is inside of me. I scoop the clear, cold water up and hours of thirst are quenched.

Once the soul is alone, all that's left is the long process of pruning. I ran this clear summer morning by the Mill River in Leeds, just down the hill from my house and usually a river I don't notice. This morning, though, it was putting on a show equal to just about anything I'd seen in a while. Dew from the hard rains of yesterday, a clear, burning sun thick on the river like gold cloth, transparent, floating shimmer. I felt the mud give under my toes as I ran. I decided not to be anywhere else.

A month after Steve died I moved back to Massachusetts from my parents' home. My mother, watching me gather up books from around her house to sell to a used bookstore, decided it was time I went home. I drove the hour-and-a-half journey holding on to the steering wheel like it was the edge of a cliff. I drove through hail and high winds. I came back to Leeds to live.

Just this summer, though, I've started to see things around here. Finally the healing has caught up with the place and I've faced those first hours I spent alone three years ago.

I FOUND THE COTTAGE in Leeds not long after Steve and I moved to Massachusetts from Colorado. It was inexpensive and set in a grove of cedars and pines. Behind the house, fields stretch in three directions. The owner of the house, Rachel, lives in a new addition, built many years later than the small red house. Our houses connect by a doorway closed off when Rachel decided to make the house into a duplex after her divorce.

Steve and I moved many times in our short marriage. Twice in Denver, twice in Aspen. And we spent those months when Steve was sick going back and forth from Connecticut to Leeds. We would pretend everything was okay. Sometimes, I could believe that we were just any ordinary couple. Steve reading in bed, his bath water growing cold as I sat by the fire, a few birds outside, light snow on the ground, sun hitting the floor here and there. Those small hours of quiet gave me hope.

One day we spent the afternoon looking at Steve's portfolio, remembering the prize-winning work he had done. Sometimes I forgot Steve's name, he was so changed, and thought, who is this?

I was cut off from my body and my mind and my heart, floating somewhere in a time just after where we had been—numb, continuing, breathing.

After Steve's death I used the house as a place to sleep. The first summer I lived here, it was hot. I worked as an intern on the magazine where he worked for two weeks before we realized how sick he was. It was the job we had moved East for, the reason we were in Leeds.

That summer I could hardly walk. I welcomed the structure of work—nine to five. In August I started to get a paycheck when I replaced an editorial assistant on vacation. I had to write everything down. For several days all I did was retype my supervisor's Rolodex, address after address on a sticky typewriter. At lunch I came home and sobbed for an hour and then went back to work.

All day I felt the press of bodies on my skin. My hands itched. The bottom of my feet itched, my belly button itched, the drums of my ears itched. I couldn't look at skin without feeling I was pulled into that flesh. I was brushed and aroused by the movement of fingers on a page, the back of a neck, the sound of one leg moving against another across the room.

I had a friend who took me out by the broken dam on

the Mill River, a town below the Williamsburg Dam that crumbled in 1874 and wiped out much of Leeds and killed 145 people.

"Houses," a newspaper report of the time states, "were taken up like kindling to crumble as ashes, trees mown down as if grass, and boulders were tossed like pebbles. The water came and swallowed up. The people on the low places were no more and the people on the high places wrung their hands."

Now the water breaks in tea-colored swatches down into the river. My friend at work told me about things that had happened to her, about her miscarriage, about the hard job of connecting again. She promised me that time does, eventually, weld itself back together. One day as I was typing, she leaned over the partition near my desk and asked, "Do you want a real job?"

I said yes, and soon after I was teaching at the college in Springfield.

IT's A CLEAN-SWEPT DAY as it sharpens. Even the butcher mentions it as he hands me my chicken, bleeding through the wrapper. In my yard the old walnuts toss their sheer-skinned leaves in the wind, warming, filaments of sun shaft their way down to the tips. Next door there are men repairing the roof of the old mansion. Slate, it must be expensive. I can hear blasts of conversation fall off the roof and smell the binding tar, like creosote.

I HAVE RUN INTO several large spiders in the gardens around the house. One is a nursery-web spider, elegant, dark, dusty brown standing guard in a messy web on top of the tiger lilies. Several of her babies have hatched, tiny filaments of other spiders encased still in their own tunnel-shaped web.

According to my guidebook, the female carries her egg sac under her body, holding the sac in her fangs until hatching time, when she builds a nursery web and suspends the sac in the threads. She waits until almost all the spiderlings have gone off. In some species the male gives the female a courtship gift of a fly.

I can work in the gardens for hours. Like the mountains, the garden wraps around and holds time until the word has no meaning. Weeds consume me, the feathers of dill. A new chocolate-colored beetle, large jagged holes in the chard. I don't think of anything when I'm bent to the vegetables. Sweat drips onto my hands as I work, the grackles keep up a chatter in the walnuts. I startle a tiny black toad.

Delicate mushrooms are fading near the transplants of lettuce. None of these facts are important but they root me once more to a place that's surrounded with manageable things. I can control the order of the garden. I can at least make it beautiful and fruitful and easy.

If I build this cultivated order around me once again, I can find, perhaps, the clues to who I am, what I listen for, the clues to why the large snapping turtle in the Mill River gives me such joy as he pulls his neck in and slides back down to the shallows when he spots me watching. I am again, for a short time, the center of the spoke. I can see the country around me. I can touch small distance.

Death has no distance, no boundaries. Its maps are territories neither wild nor cultivated. There is no language for what it is. It's the looking back from a field of sunlight to the sure cold caverns of something else. I've been trying to map death for quite a while.

The sheer motion gets you out, after all, walking back toward doing something is just about all there is. The problem is that once back, nothing is a named variety. And there are no guidebooks for a world everyone else seems to understand. So you fake it for a while, pretend you understand how things work. The post office is the place for the mail, you eat dinner around six, in the morning you put your clothes on and wash your face. Men have short hair, women have long. Parents have children, candles burn low. Lights are for the dark.

A FEW DAYS AGO I found a cedar waxwing on the grass near my house, the colors soft but clear, red tips on the buff wings, the brightest red, clear glass, no shadows. The bird is my signal for death. There's an old Irish superstition, according to two sisters I met the winter after Steve's death, that when a bird flies into the house someone in the family will die. We did not have a bird fly into the house before Steve's death but the sound of wind, like wings, followed us for months before we knew he was sick.

How long after someone you love dies can you proclaim yourself whole? I'm starting to think that there is never a completion to the body again once death cuts away from the bone. There is, rather, a sealed-off portion of the soul that heals itself over, an empty place like the center of a shell still echoing from waves, salt.

A friend whose wife died calls it his Tupperware theory.

You close each lid and go on to the next container. Step by step through your life, with no connection between the parts.

Life now is like getting up from a nap in the afternoon—a bit disoriented. Nothing like the switching of parts and names after Steve died, something milder but still sinister. An unbalance I can't quite put my finger on, the uneasiness of two o'clock with the sun so bright it washes out the color and even the grackles are silent.

I am stained, too, with mourning.

"Don't expect us to pick you up and drive you to Vermont," my mother said this morning, a residue of the months when I gripped the steering wheel on the edge of each new mile to keep the car from going out of control.

The first fall after Steve's death I drove the highway south to teach my three classes—a part-time load. I taught two composition classes and one business and technical writing class. I had never taught technical writing before, but one of my colleagues convinced me that it would be a piece of cake once I mastered the method he had perfected.

He was right but he didn't count on the geography of my life at the moment. I was still getting lost. Losing track of what year it was. Not sure why the sun was hanging above me in the sky as I passed the Holyoke Range. Shouldn't it be much lower down? I would wonder.

One day I panicked on the way into Springfield and quit the highway before I usually got off, my heart racing, arms going numb. I got lost in a muddle of streets and warehouses. I was sure I'd miss my first class that morning.

I lost my left arm whenever I taught the business and technical writing class. It just disappeared. It would hang useless by my side, numb, the numbness going all the way to my face sometimes. I was surprised the students didn't notice I was missing parts of me as I stood in front of the class.

Soon, though, I started listening to students. They told me about their lives. Often they were broken at nineteen—the same age I was when I lived in England for a year. They put themselves through school, they came from small towns and didn't understand the violence in the streets of Springfield—young boys threw bottles at them, people were knifed—their parents were getting a divorce and the father wanted to sell the house they grew up in, they were molested as children, they were black in a white school, international in a small town, angry at me for being a teacher, for being a woman, for giving them grades in January.

I stopped seeing students' eyes at night. I stayed on the highway till the last exit. I stopped teaching business and technical writing. I ran by the Mill River. I started to write again with words posted at the top of the page—river, flood, arm, light.

A MAN WHO KEEPS BEES here came today. We talked about my car, he'd like to buy one like it, and I asked him what the gooey white frames were for.

"Adding on to the hives," he said. "This way they'll make more honey."

Then he showed me black raspberries growing on the forsythia bushes. We have good ones around here because of his bees, each little sac on the berries filled out and deeply black. Each one is a flower, he told me, and with no bee activity you don't get good pollination, but here the berries are perfect.

I like to watch him garb up for the hives, elaborate protection, a hat like an old gardening hat with a veil, thick white gloves, and the zippered bee suit.

Later, out on the step, Livia, Rachel's daughter, and her friend were eating honeycomb brought to them by the beekeeper. There are two swarms, one in the old apple tree. He showed me the white combs that the bees have started to make, sleepy bees drugged with honey. He sprayed the other hive in the fir tree near the garden with sugar water and coaxed the swarm, one bee on top of another, into a new white hive for a young woman who wants to learn how to keep bees.

WHEN THE WEATHER CHANGES I shift my books from the porch to the living room and back again. I'm reading about Thoreau—the quilted matter of his life, how he worked on several projects at once, rewriting and reworking the journals and the books and the articles, how he taught himself to see differently every ten years, how he labored over the friendship with Emerson, how he stood in the mud and watched waterbugs on the stream for hours, his love of the wilderness of the brain. I'm trying to learn again that focus: how to watch bugs for hours, how to settle longer than a butterfly, how not to uproot thoughts, throw them off.

Next door at the mansion, a man is talking to another man who is above him on a porch. Yesterday at the same time the same two men were talking. Rachel and her children have come back from swimming. She has a difficult time living with two children by herself. About a year ago a man she was seeing died. He had cancer. He was thirty-six years old. Not long after that her father died. She often talks about moving, selling the house. Last fall she decided to add on a room between two sections of the house where I had planted a perennial garden. I moved the plants in freezing weather. This year she's decided to add on to the back instead.

The children's voices are softer than the man's voice next door—high and loud pleading his case with the man on the ground. The ravens are cawing above the sound of the man's voice. "What right does happiness—I mean before," he says and I lose the rest under the noise of the birds.

A FAMILY OF RACCOONS startled me this morning as I walked across the yard on my way to the post office. Smoothly silent, a mother raccoon and five babies, almost as large, dripped off the big walnut in front of the house and walked across the clipped grass into the bushes by the wall built by unemployed workers in the late 1800s. I hear the raccoons fighting at night and see their fur caught on the plastic edges of the dumpster cover.

A friend who is a traveler and a writer called last night. He said, "I think we'll come to a time when we won't need things between us and the animals, not guns or the cameras that replaced them. Just being near them will be enough."

I'm touching the backs of animals and bugs here. Killing beetles this morning, gathering them up as they mate on the furry leaves of raspberries or zinnias. I don't like killing anything but the beetles are in competition with my crops and flowers. Still, that sense that I've squeezed off life doesn't make me happy.

I admire the animals around my house. There are two battered cats who I like especially. I used to throw rocks at them to stop them from spraying my house as territory but their long hold on life finally won my respect. They are both survivors. The older is a black-and-white cat who for one whole winter lost all his hair and had a great swollen head. The other is a tabby, much more handsome than the first. He drags one leg that was gouged early in the spring.

The black-and-white cat who Rachel calls Heathcliff has been around here for at least ten years. He was out in the garden yesterday smelling the basil. I saw the tabby spraying at the edge of the tall pinewood near the cottage, lifting his tail as high as he could, a curved, yellow furl at the edge of the dark wood.

There's a chorus of crows in the walnuts each morning and fat, sleek jays who squawk at each other. A small squirrel comes each afternoon at about four to eat the berries on the wild dogwood in the front garden. I often touch raccoon fur when I dump the garbage.

These animals cheer me, so determined and knowing as they go from one task to another. A map of the territory in their animal brains. They know what they're here for. After Steve's death I lost that sense of orientation. I wasn't sure anymore who I was.

WHEN I WAS GARDENING today I found a black widow spider. I spotted her on a cluster of zinnias toward the back and watched her jump and threaten a Japanese beetle who flew off. She seemed much more furry than her picture in the guidebook, less shiny. But there was no other spider that had red markings like that.

I couldn't remember how deadly her bite was so I looked up the information in a book I have called *Medicine for Mountaineering.* The black widow (*Latrodectus mactans)* is the only spider found in the United States which is capable of routinely producing serious illness by its bite.

"The black widow alone is capable of causing a significant number of deaths among its victims. Even so, fatalities from the bite of this spider are limited almost entirely to small children or elderly individuals in poor health." The passage describes the pinprick of the bite and then an hour later the severe pain that spreads from the site of the bite through the whole body and lasts for two to four days. It takes weeks for some people to recover.

"Of all spiders," the guidebook tells me, "the black widow is the most feared. After mating, the female often eats the male, earning the name widow."

All night I dream about the black widow spider—mate eater, child killer. In the morning I run with my friend Cathy and tell her about the spider. "Oh," she says, "they were always on the south side of the house in Nevada. I just didn't let Craig play where he might get bit."

THERE HAS BEEN a study recently of survivors that seems to indicate that rehashing the past is less healthy than putting it away, forgetting about it. Who are you, though, in the present, without the past? What strings attach you to the landscape when the past of others shows up in planted groves of pines almost two hundred years old now, or a wall, or the ghosts who turn on lights around here at night?

I've been digging in the library for information about the cottage where I live and the elaborate red brick house the people around here call "the mansion." The house was started in 1879, finished in 1880. Once there were extensive gardens, no trace now, a greenhouse and a caretaker who probably lived in my cottage, a fruit orchard, a large barn, and several cows.

The brick house was built by Lucius Dimock who owned a silk company down the hill from his house. Leeds was once called Factory Village, and the first mechanical loom in America was perfected here in the early 1800s.

The Shepherd family imported merino rams from Spain, caught up in a rush on merino sheep that pushed the price of a ram up to $1,000. The first Shepherd was an industrious man and his factories still stand in Leeds, dating back to the early nineteenth century. His mill became one of the major woolen manufacturing firms in the Northeast. In 1826 the mill owned 1,400 sheep and produced 3,200 pounds of wool.

James Shepherd built the house that sits right in front of mine. It's one of the oldest houses in Leeds, built in 1812. He called it Grove Hill and planted rows of cedars and a dense forest of white pines. This fall I watched an eagle preening in first light on the tip of one of the pines.

The house was home to a succession of factory owners. One, an A. P. Critchlow, built the wall I can see from my back porch. He hired local men out of work after the flood destroyed one hundred homes and fifteen factories in 1874.

I've been thinking about the women who worked in

Mr. Shepherd's mill. Out of 118 workers, half were women. Wages for the women were lower than wages for men. Women worked in burling, linting, and marking cloth. The working hours in summer were sunrise to sunset, thirteen to fourteen hours in the mill.

When Steve was sick I imagined a box. I was in the box, the walls were very slick, I scraped the slick walls with my blunt nails. Now I've been sewn down by strings to the ground, filaments of attachment that snap and reverberate as I pull out toward the edges. I don't know how to cut the traces free.

I have planted a garden, I have a job. I have relearned vowels. I have cut my hair. Swept the barn, cared for the chickens, watered the basil, loved my family, learned how to small talk. I have swept the traces clean, and polished them, and oiled them, and called them here.

I WENT UP to a high ledge above the Connecticut River Valley last night with a man I don't know very well. We wanted to see the full moon from the ledge. The moon cupped all the light from the earth as far as we could see and poured it back on those folds and folds of mist-ridden hills.

A hawk cried once and then once again—kee, kee. Nothing else moved except the man's lips on my lips, his hands in my hair. I was attached to the ledge, to the light-dipped landscape. We stayed there for a long time, until the cold and the mosquitoes drove us off. Everything was still on the pine path to the bottom, except the wind, slightly up like a soft stream in the pines, and one call of an animal I couldn't name in the field, stalks of moon-tipped grasses just beyond the heady pines. I was frightened in a pleasant way, the earth strange for me again.

No one was up. We traversed silent roads and the trees, the leaves were all shot through with a silvery light. We thought we saw vines of white flowers in the trees. I was driving through the night I didn't know anymore, with a man I didn't know under the moon streaming out some kind of message to the hours we traversed.

I HAVE, I now realize, been masquerading here. As I drive up the hill past the house where the man and the woman and the child are on display, I know for sure that I'm a fraud. They are dismantling their house before my eyes, transforming their yard into an intricate world. This world is open to view. It consists of a white picket fence, three small gardens, one with a bench, one with vegetables shaded by a wooden canopy, and one full of annuals flowering along a stone wall I watched the man construct.

There is a line for drying clothes. Yesterday it was full of diapers. There's a swing set and a plastic pool for the baby who looks about two years old. The woman was tying up tomatoes when I went past today, her hair pulled back with a scarf. The man had a red bandanna tied across his brow and was up on the porch, scraping paint. I wondered when they were going to paint the house.

They are dug in here, a family reordering their patch of territory as I watch. I'm just making do, pretending to be here so I'll convince myself that I am here. Sometimes it doesn't work. I went off a few days ago to Vermont for a bike ride. I camped. I remembered the long, sacred time of the road. I remembered the white sky of indistinct morning. I remembered that one bird sings before all the others and then later, much later, the chorus begins. I saw the fingers of dead trees at dawn holding above the bog the imperfect webs of spiders, catching light.

I paddled around a small lake and saw kingfishers darting down to the silver surface of the water along the willows and catkins of the bank. I liked being set free from the order of the yard here.

Back in Leeds the air is so thick I swim from bed to table to bed again. The white humidity closes the world down around the edges and I can't see the Holyoke Range, that line of hills that reflects in the oxbow of the Connecticut River made famous by nineteenth century painters like Thomas Cole. Each droplet of time condenses. The ripples stop and enter my mind where they rest, churning up artifacts of the past, dislodging thoughts which startle me as I pull weeds near the chard.

I LIKE THE IDEA of the music of the spheres, time's winged chariot, the underworld, all the contraptions of myth, but sometimes I can't place these notions in the flat surface that extends around me. There's a lot of activity but not much I can hang on to. Cold mountain water is there, the fingers on my hand are there, the squirrel testing the roof is there, but most everything else is symbol. Those shadows on someone's wall.

In the garden nothing is what it isn't. An ant is the complicated life of the ant, the lettuce only lettuce rubbed with dew, the dirt breaking down nourishing. The elements all there to catalog—earth, air, water, fire.

On my desk I have two postcards from an exhibit of Georgia O'Keeffe's work I saw last year. She seems to have had a knack for seeing the other side—cow's skull and calico rose, horrible and beautiful, at peace, full of death, sensuous, on the edge. In *Red Hills and Bones*, the bones in the foreground are as massive as the hills, struck by the contours of light.

Her landscapes were mapped with that terrible splendor, some kind of spiritual connection I can't find anymore. She understood her own version of space and death. I'd like to be there, at the center of my own spoke and wheel, where I can touch hard elements of unnamed nothingness.

When I was in college in Maine a student was murdered. Someone got off the highway and killed her early one morning. I stopped walking alone late at night. The boundaries around my landscape tightened. Not long after the murder, I went out to the pond behind my dorm where the willows were that deep color of late fall at dusk. I wanted to find out why. I believed there were answers.

Mist was rising from the pond, the edges of clipped grass, the bending slashes of the willows. I was surrounded by beauty and reason. I felt the world was a whole, a seamless ordered place. Even the murder was part of this. It was somehow bound up in the beauty. I felt the presence of something good and healing, encompassing. I knew things were okay in some indefinable way of the universe.

When Steve's dad was dying, I asked Steve if he was all

right. He said yes, he thought that everything was part of a whole, it all made some kind of crazy sense, we were all meant to go back to dust, and corn and grass.

I can't pull things together the way I did years ago by the pond in Maine. Maybe I'm not asking the right questions. I just come up on boxed walls. I thread my way into the present only to be sucked back to the past. Yesterday I tried to play a tape that Steve recorded several years before I met him, talking about his work. I took it to the car and tried to rewind it.

No sound came out when I pressed the play button. When I ejected the tape I could see that the plastic had snapped.

Mourning is churned up like still water. Easy stones thrown from the bank. Just the toe of something sets it off again—that reverberation of loss. Each step out into the world responds with a tightening of the chords of loss. It's hard to give up that last center of pain, cut off mostly unnoticed; it seems to hold some of the last touches of Steve.

A friend told me a story yesterday about her neighbor. A man who had watched her ten-year-old son off and on, someone who had a key to her home and was just about to start painting her century-old farmhouse white.

I read about him in the newspaper. A week ago, he broke into a woman's house in Williamsburg and raped her, robbed her, and beat her up. The woman was sixty-five years old. He had warned people that if he ever had anything to drink again he'd go crazy. He was married for the past six years to a woman he had met at an AA meeting. She had two children who lived with them. He was a nice guy. My friend and her husband trusted him. Everyone knew he had been in jail and had murdered someone, but they believed, my friend told me, that he had turned his life around.

THE WATER WAS TEA-COLORED this morning when I took my shower. Once again I ran out of hot water. I walked down to the post office and met up with a man I often see walking around here. He tilts when he walks, his cutoffs are spattered with paint, and the old green sweatshirt he wears has a streak of red across the back. He's started nodding to me as we pass on the road to the post office. When I get back from the post office I walk around the garden. Rachel and the children are gone, so even her section of the house is quiet.

In the mail this morning was a thank-you note from a friend who was just married. Her wedding was in the church where Steve and I were married. Some of the same people were there. During the ceremony, my sister and I were sitting together and halfway through the long Catholic wedding I knew I was in trouble. I was convinced I was going to explode.

"Eat this mint," Mary Jean whispered. "Don't do anything stupid."

When Steve was sick, Mary Jean had a hard time dealing with everything.

"It was those marks on his head that really bothered me," she told me this summer. "I wanted to design a way that they wouldn't have to leave the ink on like that."

IT'S DIFFICULT TO CONCENTRATE on life. Death comes in the small box at the post office, it creeps through conversations, relatives each day dole out the new hours of death. My Aunt Carol's mother is dying.

"She has that look," Carol said yesterday. Her mother is dying of cancer. Carol has just gone through a good part of a year of treatments for her own cancer.

Granta's latest issue is called "Death," and this morning I flipped open to a series of deathbed photographs. Horrible, chilling images—no warmth left in the hands, or the features, just death—not peaceful, just there.

Some of Thoreau's last words were "one world at a time," which he spoke in answer to a curious preacher's question about what things looked like from the brink of the dark river. The concentric circles of Steve's life and death continue to overlap and undercut my experiment to live in the present. It's a lack of concentration and focus, chopping out the echoes.

Bird song, bird chatter delineates my boundaries these days, waking me in the morning, calling out at night when I think everything should be sleeping. The spring peepers are gone and I can't remember hearing the cicadas lately. Cars pull across the bird chatter. A hummingbird flaps in that whirring way on the impatiens, the geraniums. Her mimic— the hummingbird moth—sucks nectar from the bee balm in the front garden. The muggy air holds the leaves down, tips pulling toward the ground, crows eat mulberries. Each hour is still caught up with a sense of loss in the back of my mind, a pinprick of recognition, small, undramatic, constant.

Not long ago I walked on a road I used to walk almost every day when I lived in Vermont. It was a cool lane in summer, spare and full of the tatters of beech leaves in cold Novembers, and a good place to ski all winter. One of those abandoned New England thoroughfares, the Cowshed Road, stood unchanged for the twenty years I knew it. Now the far side of the road has been improved, electricity strung, three houses already finished and more to come.

A few years ago my Uncle Bill, visiting from Boise, took a photograph of a shady section of the road, slashed with white birch; it hangs in his living room in Idaho. Carol, his wife, had never seen the road and wanted to walk there. I warned her that things had changed, but still she found it beautiful, and, after all, the section photographed was still the same.

I'm trying not to feel these losses of territory and landscape as much as I used to. The first time I saw a pileated woodpecker was on the Cowshed, ragged, imperial in size. I heard the chopping first and then saw the bird. A few months ago I saw a pileated woodpecker from the windows here, where I write. Same ragged stance, skinny regal bird.

I don't want the landscape to change but it does, often with violence and in irrevocable ways. The order I once thought was underneath all this has to be given a new name, reordered, reconvinced. I need a new vocabulary, a new way to think about the world, the word. I need to touch the sandy bottom of the streambed with my lips, understand origins and destination. I need to redefine loss and refind ecstasy, dust off the crust of the last three years.

There's a bird calling right now, a kind of round purr, high pitched, thick. A buzz with a flare. The wind's got itself up a bit to ruffle the walnut leaves and send a ripple through the room. I continue to miss the snapping turtle in the Mill River.

WHERE DO THE SEEDS of renewal come from? I'm looking at a small watercolor. It sits on my desk, framed in rosewood. It was painted by a Chinese artist in a rainswept booth at a festival called Chinese Osterley at a historic house outside of London. I bought it for about ten dollars. I decided when I was almost at the gate of the grounds that I had to buy it, and I rushed back through the mud and rain to find the little booth. It was the first time after Steve's death, a year before, that I could see celebration and color.

In the painting you can see mist drops on the watercolor, smudges of white on the misty crags of mountains. The painter has a narrow boat in the middle distance, reflected in the water where it looks like dawn is washing itself clear. Mountain, water, boat, one single tree, and windswept rain from another place pointing the wash of blues and grays.

The watercolor is my talisman. Painting a foreign landscape from history and memory under the shelter of a red-canopied booth in the windswept English rain, mixture of paint and desire, framed in time. A reordering of concentration in the weather. A rebinding of the soul, print of distance in a brush on paper, the silent boat, the reflected crags in the mist, the waters of the air, and the paint pot. A desire to see again.

7

Forest on the moraines, sagebrush on the outwash plains—
that is the rule, and the situation is due to the underlying
terrane. The moraines consist of heterogeneous rock materials
carried out from the range by the ancient glaciers. Because of
their compactness they retain the moisture essential to forest
growth: they are also rich in minerals that are likewise
necessary. Quite different are the plains. Largely made up
of quartzite cobbles spread over the valley by glacial streams
that formerly flowed in from the north, the plains are
both barren and dry.
FRITIOF FRYXELL, *The Tetons,*
Interpretations of a Mountain Landscape

A few hours ago I was kissing a man in a garage in Florida. He's interested in my breasts and my thighs and my lips—not my familiar ghosts. One night we went to the beach, later I had pink sand pooled in my ears. Widow. Antonia Fraser tells me in her book *The Weaker Vessel* that widows in seventeenth century England were often happy and powerful—they had their dead husband's riches, but they were free to do what they wanted. They were in charge of their lives unlike women who were married or single at that time. I am trying to cultivate a new lightness I'm feeling. I, too, would like to be powerful.

Now I write at the rim of the world, perched on the edge of the elk preserve in Kelly, Wyoming. I've flown here from Florida after a week visiting my parents for Christmas. They spend the winter in the south now, the summer in Vermont. The cabin is warm. Orion, my companion—a silky orange cat—sits on my lap as I write. The sky shines above us with all the burning stars in this world and the next.

It's January, and I've come to Wyoming to try to write the preface for my collection of poetry as part of the last project for my doctorate. I have two weeks to write before I fly home to Massachusetts. Ted is renting a cabin above the town now, and he invited me to spend a couple of weeks here while he travels. He keeps the trailer in Kelly as his office and I'm in charge of that too.

I write at a window that looks east over the sage-pricked snow to a bluff above the town. If I turn north I see the ragged tips of the Tetons; west, the round curves of the hills rolling across the national elk preserve.

We had a thaw for the past week or so, and now I can watch the icicles disintegrate along the edge of the roof. If I walk down off the bluff I can see north across the flat plains where moose winter all the way to the horizon. Mountains rim the landscape. Clouds sweep across the luminous winter sky outside. In the morning at seven, I watch the full moon set. I am washed with a clarity.

Once, a long time ago, I stayed in a cabin like this not far from here with my brother and sister. My parents were in their own cabin. It was the last part of a long trip we took to the West. We saw all the important places. My brother and I rode donkeys down into the Grand Canyon and slept at a ranch on the bottom. I was fifteen and afraid of our guide, an old man who kept telling me he wanted to kiss me. My brother promised to protect me.

But the cabin at Jenny Lake was our favorite place. Even my mother and father went riding when we were there. I remember climbing high up into the mountains, silver water streaming off the horses' legs as we crossed shallow rivers.

How much have I changed, I wonder, as I struggle over the words I type each day on scrap sheets of paper. Who was I at fifteen, seeing mountains for the first time, tasting mountain water, washing my face in the cold stream.

My parents warned me that if I leave my job and my furniture, they won't buy me a new couch again. I had a violent argument with them at Christmas. I suggested I might try to have a child by myself.

"You're crazy," my mother said.

I'm paid much less than the men in my department, but my friend has told me not to ask for a raise until she gets hers. I can barely remember who I was two years ago when I was in Kelly.

I have certain chores: water the plants, keep Orion fed and happy, check the trailer down in Kelly now and then, bring the garbage over to Mr. Kent's, service the car before I leave.

This morning I went to dump the garbage and pick up more kitty litter at the trailer, and I couldn't get the car to start. Once I did (the car is a twenty-year-old Datsun patched with duct tape) I couldn't get enough traction to make it up the first hill. So I set out to put the chains on. I couldn't remember how to attach the jack to the car or how to fasten the chains. I put the chains back into the car and tried once more to gun it up the slippery hill. First gear, I realized, works better than second.

I am not quite sure what is safe. Sometimes I feel as if my life is like that, precariously balanced, the definitions of how to be, or how not to be, confused.

I'm reading fairy tales. In one of the tales of the Brothers Grimm, "The Juniper Tree," translated by Lore Segal, a husband and wife want a child. For a long time they can't have one. The man is rich; the wife is beautiful and good. The woman wishes for a child "as red as blood and as white as the snow." She stands under the juniper tree in their front yard.

Spring comes, the woman is pregnant, she eats the fruit of the juniper tree and gets sick. She says to her husband, "When I die bury me under the juniper tree." She has a baby—a boy as red as blood and as white as the snow. She is so happy, she dies. Her husband buries her under the juniper tree and cries and cries and cries for a long time until one day he stops. After that he takes a new wife.

They have a daughter and the new wife grows very jealous of the son and plots to get the whole fortune for her daughter. She sets up Ann Marie so she thinks she has knocked her brother's head off and killed him.

Ann Marie cries and cries but the mother says, "Keep quiet, we'll stew him in a sour broth." Ann Marie cries into the pot "so that it didn't need any salt."

The father comes home and keeps asking, "Where is my son?"

"He's gone on a trip to visit his mother's great uncle," the woman tells her husband. And the father eats the stew the wife has made. Ann Marie cries, and the husband says, "What good stew this is." He eats all the food and then throws the bones under the table.

Ann Marie scoops them up and puts them in her best silk scarf, weeping tears of blood. She takes them out and lays them under the juniper tree. This makes her feel better.

The juniper tree moves its branches back and forth like clapping and then a beautiful bird flies out of the mist that's come up. The bird flies first to the roof of a goldsmith and then to a cobbler and then to a mill. At all three he sings the same song and sings it so well he bargains for gifts: a gold chain, shoes, and a millstone.

The bird sings: "My mother she butchered me, my father he ate me, my sister, little Ann Marie, she gathered up the bones of me and tied them in a silken cloth to lay under the juniper. Tweet twee, what a pretty bird am I!"

The bird comes back to the rich man's house and sings his song. The song makes the father happy, his wife stops up her ears, Ann Marie cries and cries. The father goes outside and the bird drops the gold chain around his neck. Ann Marie goes out to see if she has a present too, and the bird throws the shoes down to her. She puts on the red shoes and dances into the house.

The woman is frantic, her hair "standing on end like flaming fire." She goes outside and the bird throws the millstone on her head and kills her. Steam and flames rise up and the bird becomes the boy and the family goes inside to eat supper.

I like this tale, the elements of resurrection and resolution after great loss cheer me in some strange way.

I SKIED down by the Gros Ventre River. Before he left, Ted said there was a road there that ran along by the water. I couldn't find the road, but followed a bluff for a while which brought me very close to a moose. I didn't have my glasses on, so I had to judge by his size, the shape of his antlers, the way he moved across the snow, large body suspended on small legs. I had heard that moose are easily angered and they'll attack if they feel threatened, so I dropped down and skirted closer to the river where there was a rangy thicket of cottonwoods and a cluster of mule deer browsing the brush.

I thought about skiing up behind the cabin into the elk preserve, but some of the slopes looked avalanche prone. I like being surrounded by something beautiful I don't quite trust. I walked along the ridge, like moving in a symphony. Each element one after the other and together—raven, coyote, wind, hill, snow, sage, river-sweep, mountain, cloud, sun, moon. I noticed what I finally decided were moose tracks. Two sets, one almost directly on top of the other. I felt their tracks with the tips of my fingers in the road.

Pine fences run off the curve of fields perfectly positioned. Tips of sagebrush shadow on the snow when the sun moves out along the edge of clouds. I stopped at a place where I could see both the town of Kelly, north of the river, and the blue bends of the Gros Ventre twisting through cottonwoods and birch, aspen groves. Right where I stopped I saw the moose. She matched the browns of the brush, but her shape was unmistakable—large drooping chest and the pendulous head. She swung her legs back and forth to uncover grasses to eat. Below her, closer to the river, was another smaller moose. Perhaps the two sets of tracks I saw on the road.

"They like walking on the road," Ted told me. "It's easier for them than the snow."

Did they go down to the river to drink and eat? Are they the same moose who live on this ridge? A raven watched me watching the moose. Later I saw her fly past, ragged regal wings, her mouth full of something white. In the bluffs to the south the coyotes were yipping as the sun pulled itself farther down. I watched the hills soften and break.

Today, waiting for a storm, I decide to put the chains on the car so I can get out tomorrow if it snows. I have been sick for two days and my eye is red and swollen. I've given up trying to type. I think I might have to go to a doctor. Not a simple task if I'm snowed in, so I position the car at the brow of the road and try to get the chains on. I know I have one of the hooks wrong, but I'm hoping they will hold until the main road where I can take the chains off.

Later, I walk along the road. I'm not expecting the moose. I stop at the same spot on the ridge just to check out the river and the town to see if I can see Gary's car. I am wondering if I should tack a note to his door to tell him I'm back in Kelly. And then I see the moose.

Their browsing spot is in the cottonwoods, at the edge of the deep blue river that curves against the bluff where I stand. I watch the two brown bodies, prehistoric on the landscape that stretches north up the flat basin cupped by the surrounding mountains.

I admire animals. There is no question of place, no learning to see again, to speak again for a moose, or at least not as far as I can tell. Just that concentration on eating the right grass, on swinging your leg back and forth so the large, heavy hoof will uncover the wet grass, on drinking from the river, on sleeping.

THE NEXT DAY when I try to start the car, it's dead. I left the door open a crack yesterday. I snap on my skis and push myself through the snow down across the hills to Kelly. I am fragile and cold. Once in town, I take off my skis and walk toward Ted's trailer looking for someone who might help me jump-start the car.

"You might ask Lee Donaldson at the post office," one man in a ski jacket tells me after he hands me a package for Ted. I drop the package off at the trailer and walk over to the post office.

"Try Herb," the postmaster says. "He's probably home now and he doesn't have much to do."

"Sure," Mr. Lux says when I ask if he can help me, and he drives me up the long road to the Datsun in his large white Oldsmobile and starts the car after several tries.

I GIVE UP TRYING to write the preface. Later, I take the advice of one of my committee members who says, "Pretend you're writing for a smart student in a freshman class. Don't do anything fancy."

I've been consumed by words these past months. Sometimes I forget where I am as I walk around the streets of Leeds. Once I thought I was crossing a river in Vermont as I drove from Hadley to Northampton on the other side of the Connecticut River. I wonder if my confusion is a sign of the dislocation of my spirit.

Here, in Wyoming, I'm too sick to do much except watch. I can't retrace my steps to contentment. I'm tired of waiting for the weather to clear, for my cold to run its course, for the directions to the rest of my life to appear like magic on the kitchen counter one morning after I've slept well under a heavy elk skin. I make a list of small accomplishments. I keep checking my face in the large mirror in the bedroom. I stare back at myself, the hard curve of an elk horn curling near my ear, a trophy Ted has hauled into the cabin.

I DREAM SOMETIMES about a man who takes me out to the forest and chops out my heart first, and then stands there eating it as I watch. There are several blue jays flying around and the air is very still. I'm not afraid. This has happened before. I see my face in a mirror hung on one of the trees and it looks familiar, lined and scarred. So that's why I mutter, the closer he comes to finishing the more I wonder what he'll do next. My heart is tough, it doesn't make him happy, so he starts one by one to eat the folds of my brain. I don't really care anymore, this is the forest after all and everything is supposed to end happily someday, so I figure before he eats his fill something wonderful will happen, won't it? The jays will fly off, the air will clear and the man I loved but lost will come back and rescue me from this man who is eating my brain, putting a bit of pepper here, a dash of salt there, but doesn't know what it tastes like any more than I do.

AFTER TWO WEEKS I fly home and put my skis away in the hot water closet on the porch in the cottage in Leeds and finish the preface. I find a woman from France to help me with my translation project. I am working on some poems in Quebecois. We sit at her kitchen table in a house not far from my office. We debate the meanings of words. I try to make my English versions as darkly beautiful as the originals. We eat chocolate cookies and drink tea. We talk about Boston and about children. She smokes and I eat another cookie.

My friend Irene has written to say her second baby is a girl and her name is Teleri. I last visited her in Wales three years ago when her first baby was only a few weeks old. She sent photographs and has invited me to stay in the bothy, a stone house that's empty now.

I've decided to go to Wales again this summer. I imagine selling my furniture, quitting my job, breaking all the attachments I've cultivated over the past three years. I want to rise up out of the limbo of my life at the present moment.

In the Breton lai "Sir Orfeo," a medieval version of the Orpheus story, Queen Heurodis sleeps by a grafted tree and is taken away by fairies who tell her husband, the king, that they will tear her apart if he tries to stop them. He wanders for ten years trying to find her. One day he sees a hunt, lords and ladies riding past in splendid attire. He laughs in delight and then sees his wife, who is taken off by her companions once again. He's clever, though, and talented, and he sings his way into the fairy court. Once there he wins her back. They return to their kingdom and live happily ever after.

I imagine the queen, before the king arrives at the hunt, learning to accept her solitude. She liked it at times, I think, her body just asleep under the leafy hot branches of noon, perched on the edge of here and then. The still breath of the next life held off by the weight of her body on the grass.

I want the queen to be the one to laugh, to be the one to break the spell of the fairies where everything is repeated—each day the hunt progressed as it had the day before, the prey flashing through the spiny columns of new oaks, no sun, just the mild, milky sky of where she always was just before morning, just as the birds begin to sing, the hawk about to break into flight.

8

I slept all night listening to the sound of the stream. Now I hear Irene calling her husband David awake from the house. Light comes through me as I turn against the mattress. I smell the heat on wet leaves near the door. Soon I hear the crunch of gravel as David goes to let the chickens out. I sleep and read in a small stone house in the north of Wales that David has reconstructed. It is June.

The house is, perhaps, three hundred years old. From my bed, suspended above the main room on a loft, I look out across the room to a landscape of white rounded walls which follow the contour of the stones. The wooden windows are open to the outside air now that the weather has cleared.

Light comes to me often here, pure, a bit yellow, old light remembered from somewhere else. Beauty is commonplace each morning. Elements placed like a gift for me on the stones outside the bothy. Air, water, light, sun, one bird dipping into the shallow pond that almost touches the house. Her long yellow-and-gray tail flicks up and down.

How powerful I feel as I throw the covers off and climb down my ladder to the stone floor. The water in the stone basin is very cold as I wash my face. I leave the door open when I walk toward the house for breakfast.

I sleep late here. It's nine o'clock as I walk around David's office, which juts out along the little stream, to the table set on the east side of the main house. The stones of the house are not painted on the east side; their rough gray glows in this light. David is pouring tea into pottery cups. Berries Irene picked yesterday are glistening in the blue bowls.

"Why aren't there any windows on this side of the house?" I ask David as I pour the warm sheep's milk onto my cereal and toss a few red currants into the bowl.

"They just didn't put them in," David says. "I like the simplicity, but it would have been nice to have some there."

He's an architect working on drawings for a college housing project that take their heft and presence from this wall. I like David's view of things. His quietly cantankerous vision.

Irene comes around the corner of the house holding Teleri. Trystan, who is three, follows. Irene moves gracefully in her bright skirt.

"Good morning," she sings out. "Did you sleep well?" She sits beside David on the wooden plank with a pillow propped behind her back against the stone wall. The baby cries and Irene suckles her. I have wanted a baby for some time now. In April it was four years since Steve's death.

Irene has been teaching me how to milk sheep. She has two sheep she milks in the shed northeast of the bothy where I sleep. I grab the teat too tightly and get only a small stream of warm milk, sticky on my hand. On the other side of the sheep, Irene squirts milk in a series of spurts into the plastic jug.

"Is it okay if I get junk in the milk?" I ask, as pieces of hay fall from my hand into my jug.

"Oh, I strain it anyway," she answers. Her container is half filled. "It took me quite a while to learn how to do this," she says. But I don't believe her.

The last time I tried milking an animal was years ago in Norway. I remember the hot teat of the cow, how soft and warm it felt in my hand, and the light coming into the barn through spattered windows.

As we milk Enid, she butts her head against the wood of the stall. "It's okay Enid," Irene croons, "we're almost finished."

WHEN IRENE FINISHES feeding Teleri she hands her to me and I hold her while Irene eats. I touch her small feet, I look into her eyes, and I follow the sun as it moves across her face. When she's hungry she nuzzles me until she's frustrated and either cries or stuffs her hand into her mouth. The last time I was here, Trystan was a tiny baby and I held him, too, bound in the crook of my arm.

Children have redefined the heft of things. Irene's day is split with the management of children. Always skilled at putting things together, she's organized a play group in Llanfrothen, the town near their farm. The group meets at the school hall two days a week. When Trystan is at the play group, Irene drives a few miles to Croeser, a tiny village over the hills, and has a massage.

David leaves most of the child care to Irene. He'll hold

the baby until she cries and then pass her to me. He'll say, "Take her, will you?" and stride off to his studio where his architectural firm designs projects in England and Wales. Irene and David met at a meeting for nuclear disarmament in a village near their farm. Children complicate politics, the focus changes.

I see the compost heap here as political. The dead duck from a month ago is tossed on the pile with the night soil from my toilet, garden weeds, kitchen garbage. There's an attempt here to circle back, make things whole. A line of movement follows the action through to consequence. History takes on a new texture. The present responds to past and future, bends a certain way because of the press of time.

When we finish breakfast, Irene goes off to a picnic with the children and David and I decide to work in the gardens. His series of beds is both beautiful and productive. The vegetable garden is off to the left of the cottage where I sleep— thick now with lettuce and potatoes and broad beans. Off toward the front pasture there's an herb garden growing wild against a stone wall and below that, the orchard. East of the main house in a terrace are two wedge-shaped plots where we'll prepare the ground for planting.

"I thought you might use this tool and break up the weeds like this," he says. And he jumps down and starts to chop and tug at the patch he cut yesterday, cleared of wheat.

The tool he uses looks easy to maneuver. Until I, too, jump down and start to jab it into the soil and pull clumps of weeds toward me on the slope.

"Where'd you get this—mattock—is it?"

"Oh, Birmingham, I think, but a long time ago—you probably couldn't get one there now."

Suddenly I've got the hang of it. I lift the smooth, carved wood up a bit and then bring the three-pronged iron down into the dark soil, loosening up the roots of pigweed and witchgrass and I pull. I don't have to stoop. I relax and work up a rhythm across the first row. Soon my hands are blistered. Sweat runs down between my breasts; my legs ache.

David is below me on another field, cutting the rough hay with a machine Trystan calls "the horrible machine." Its blades are tough enough to go through the rough grass and reeds, but the noise slashes through the silence otherwise broken only now and then by the boom of air force jets swooping in low.

I'm not thinking of anything for a while. I want to finish the upper garden before lunch, so I keep moving from row to row producing long piles of weeds as I work. I wonder what it would be like to have a place like this. Irene calls her farm a small holding.

Harald has offered me this sort of life. Before I left for Wales, he called me at home. He said he wanted our child to be an athlete. He talked about how he would start training at an early age. He even suggested that we live part of the year apart and send the child back and forth between Båteng and Massachusetts.

"You can spend the winter with your family," he said.

I had promised him that I would spend the summer in Norway after I graduated from the University of Denver. He asked me to come to Båteng this summer to work on various projects.

"Ah yes, you can help with my berry bushes," he told me when I spoke with him in the spring. "For five years I have wanted to do something with them."

When I was in Norway the first time, all those years ago, we had staked out a plot for cloudberries to grow. The delicious transparent orange berries grow wild, but are fickle, some seasons never ripening because of the cold weather.

When he called again, I told him I would not be coming to Norway this summer.

"I don't want to marry you," I said finally. "I don't want to have your child." I was surprised to hear my voice. I wasn't sure why I decided to tell Harald this now. I think I knew then that I didn't love him.

"Ah," he said, "I see, Sharon." And after a long silence, he said, "I am very disappointed."

"I'm so sorry, Harald."

"Good-bye, Sharon," he said, and I hung up the phone. He was off to check the salmon nets at midnight with his father. I could see him leaving his office, shutting the door. Putting on his jacket and walking with his father to the river's edge where they would get into the narrow black boat and push themselves out to the nets. If they were lucky, there would be a salmon, a very large and beautiful salmon caught in the sweep of net across the Tana River. And Harald would club the fish and place it in the bottom of the boat. Later he would gut it and freeze it. The midnight sun would be low in the sky and burning with a clear brilliance.

It was late afternoon and I felt empty. I went out to the

garden and sat on a plastic chair in the middle of a bed of wild blue iris. I watched the bees, their legs thick with pollen, move from one flower to the next.

My mother was relieved. She didn't want me to move to the far north of Norway. A friend of hers had been praying for months at different holy places that I would not marry Harald. We had been talking about marriage for almost three years. I missed his calls.

As I work I wonder if I made the right decision. I concentrate on the dry, crumbly soil, the way I can switch hands to move from one row to another, how I brace my legs against the toughest weeds.

David has finished cutting the grass. I move to the last patch of the plot. He starts to rake and gather the weeds. I'm now in a section riddled with roses, the last roots of parsley. I can taste salt on my skin. Each pore of my body breathes. I can't remember who I am, where I came from, what my sorrows are. I keep thinking about water with a slice of lemon, a few ice cubes. I know David won't stop now until we're finished.

Work is part of the fabric of the days here. We're in the gardens today because it's Saturday. During the week there are other tasks to complete. David's office fills by ten—he's working by a few minutes after nine, sitting at his drafting table near the window. Last week I went in to ask about a reservation at a mountain hotel. He looked up. I knew it was dangerous to interrupt—he was in the middle of putting meticulous dots on a drawing for a project he's doing for Cambridge University.

"Can you do dots?" he asked.

David's one of the few people I know who moves through his days with a kind of fierce integrity for the whole. He hardly ever compromises. Now he finds that he's spending too much time at his work and wants to cut back to a thirty-hour week so he can spend more time with Irene and the children. And spend more time designing instead of implementing the work.

One night after we've eaten a dinner of omelets—made of eggs from the chickens who live in the hut beyond the bothy, onions, broad beans, peas from the garden below—David asks Ben, a woman who has worked for him for about a year, if she would take charge of more of the projects. Ben has been telling us about Malaysia where she grew up. "I don't understand the signs now," she says, "the language has changed so much."

When Irene and David were gone and I was alone, I spent some time sitting in the sun, reading. I found a plastic chair with a thick fiberfill cushion in the closet near the bothy. It was a wonderful chair to read in and I sat there for hours watching Adrian, a man who is insulating the main house, move back and forth between the workroom and the stone house with pieces of wood. For a while Adrian's dog, a Border collie, would sit with me beside the cold, little stream.

"That's a great chair," I said to Irene when she returned.

"Oh," she said, "that was my mother's chair. David doesn't like it, doesn't think it fits in with the rest of the things, so I've ordered a new chair for my birthday."

Irene's work starts early—sometimes she lets the chickens out and then milks her two milking sheep. She strains the milk and brings a fresh jug into the house for breakfast. David's usually up in the garden, picking berries.

"My life is very different from what I thought it would be," she tells me as we drive back from taking the children up the cog railway to the top of Snowdon. The road twisting through oak woods' spotted light.

"What did you think you'd be doing?"

"Oh, something in a city, some kind of social work like the community center for the church, not so isolated as what I do now."

She sees herself in a community and her fledgling sheep business as the kind of work which fits into that community. For a while she commuted to Caernarfon, a town almost an hour away, and then she worked in the village store and post office. Now she's trying to figure out how she can get by without a car. But the walk into town is two miles and that would cut into other projects.

I met Irene a long time ago in Oxford. I was there for my junior year of college and we met at Manchester College on the first day of term. It was early October and I was nineteen. Once I got to know her better, I admired her knack for making do, transforming simplicity into elegance in the way she dressed, tied a scarf, or entertained in her room above a garage that looked out on a garden where I would sleep out some nights, drinking in the smell of roses.

I visited Irene in Dominica several years later when she was working as a volunteer in the VSO, a British organization similar to the Peace Corps. There, too, she managed to make small things seem perfect. We drank from calabashes and ate crawfish caught in the river near where we had lunch.

A few nights ago I stripped a chicken to make curry. Irene came in from shutting the chickens in their pen and examined the carcass. "I'll see what else I can get off," she said and tore the bird apart, accumulating a pile of meat. "In Dominica," she said, "they boil the bones for two days, getting every last bit."

The garden is carefully tended. In the morning we eat the fresh picked berries, sometimes strawberries a bit white, the shiny black and red currants, the raspberries, soft like the muzzle of a horse. At noon I watch David walk past the window of the bothy on his way to gather white radishes, lettuce and peas, and broad beans. He carries an oval basket.

In the evening we usually eat potatoes dug just an hour before, boiled with butter, lettuce unadorned, and the other vegetables stirred up in the wok with olive oil and herbs.

I have a notion that I want all this for myself so I try to pick up the methods. I wonder if I could do it alone. At home in Massachusetts, I garden, rent a small house, try to follow through—but I'm not all that successful. I don't preserve the vegetables. I have no compost heap. I watch television. My sins are manifold. I forget what it's like to eat outside, how the potato tastes. I don't go camping anymore. I close myself off to a community. I become preoccupied with the animals who live near me—spiders in the house, hummingbirds in the garden, the woodchuck who eats the ripe peaches in August.

I keep a map of this hillside in Wales in the corner of my mind. It stays there, protected, a refuge, a sure thing. I rely on Irene and David to keep up the good work. I need to know that this kind of life can still be had.

I was at a meeting a few nights ago where the talk was all about cultivation. A different sort of work but the same kind of impulse—stirring up the ground to plant new seeds. Irene is involved in a movement started a few years ago to connect new immigrants to Wales, who for the most part don't speak Welsh, with Welsh speakers.

The group was made up of native Welsh speakers like Irene and a man who was the former chair of the committee, English immigrants who were Welsh learners, other immigrants who were fluent in the language, and a few people who knew a smattering of words.

The idea is to connect the two groups of people to preserve the Welsh language and culture by education instead of confrontation. A gentle persuasion to change such things as the tourist pamphlets in Portmadoc now printed in English, or the signs in the Welsh craft center, all in English, or according to several committee members, the often "atrocious" Welsh translations in brochures and pamphlets, all put out by the tourist industry. The group was searching for a name at this meeting.

The members want to promote more Welsh speakers in establishments like Leo's, a slick, large new store in Portmadoc. Their manifesto is to foster a respect for Welsh culture, language, history, literature that goes beyond the familiar image of women in tall black hats.

The ten or so people at the meeting discuss ways to integrate the language, as well as ways to help learners feel more connected and thus more responsible for the culture—

keepers of the culture. We sit around a rectangular table in the almost-empty hall in Blaenau. White walls, wooden benches pushed against the walls. I take notes on the Formica top of the table.

There are several women—a doctor from Portmadoc who smiles at me as I write, the two English women who drove with us to the meeting, and a large woman from Australia.

"The Welsh are very good," one man says, "at discussing things."

And another of several older men says in Welsh that he would be happy to switch back and forth from one language to the other. Irene translates for the three of us who have learned only a few words in Welsh. This gets to be too distracting at the small table. The speakers switch for the most part to English. This irks the woman from Australia and a younger man who leans over the table and speaks only in Welsh throughout the meeting.

"We want awareness to underlie what we do—the point is to get a groundswell going, till the fields, put the manure in," says the man they have chosen to be the next chair. He's a retired minister whose wife, he tells me later, is a paraplegic.

"I didn't want to be chairman you know. I think the young people should lead this."

"The point is," he says as we stand outside the church later, roses blooming along the fence, "that just by meeting like this we're doing something. We are making a community."

Irene disagrees and has offered to do two canvassing projects that will further cut into her day. "If the talk goes nowhere," she says later, "the words must result in actions."

Jan Morris in her book *The Matter of Wales* discusses the Welsh woman's quality of character. She describes a series of exploits by women in Welsh history like Gwenllian in 1136 who led her own army against the Normans.

I'M ON THE SECOND PATCH of knotty weeds by now. My arms ache. I've watched the sun swing through the trees, the sky scrubbed clear after weeks of rain.

Steve has been dead four years and I've come to understand there is no healing—if healing is a clean slate. It's sewing up the past, learning how to carry it with you. Something lets go eventually, some broken part unhinges itself, drops off—but the release equals loss once more. My love for Steve becomes part of this story that's always pivoting on the present where he isn't.

Death has become as ordinary as work to me. Work is like death, turning the roots up, pulling the weeds across the soil to the pile. Ordinary death dispatches itself through the clods. Everyone here has lost someone—a mother, a father, a husband, a child. A man calls whose wife committed suicide a year ago.

"She went out to the garden," Irene tells me, "and hung herself while her children were at school. She was in love with another man and couldn't face it."

"Couldn't she have done something else?" I ask. "I mean, have an affair or get divorced or something?" I hear later of another mother who drowns herself in a hotel bathtub.

Drama makes its way to the house, shunting against us like waves. Irene's in the middle of some of it. The rest of us watch. A man who runs the shop in town is in love with a woman who works at the shop. This woman has left her husband. The husband had threatened to shoot Lenny and beats the wife up in the shop when Lenny isn't there. Irene has invited Jane to live in the bothy. David objects.

"He doesn't like her perfume, he doesn't like her voice," Irene tells me.

I'VE COME TO A PATCH where the soil isn't worked as much. I bring the mattock down as hard as I can into the earth. Hacking away at the roots. I'm thinking about sex. I'm thirty-seven years old. I have, I figure, six more years to have a baby.

Yesterday I hayed a field with Irene and her friend Gwen. The children were playing in a pool near the bothy and the babies were positioned in prams under a tree near the two ponies, Patch and Katie. We could hear the sheep calling to their lambs.

Patch is sick. He can't eat fresh grass so we scooped up the fresh cut hay and tossed it over the fence where he can't reach it. My job was to rake the hay into piles with a hay rake—a large wooden rake with separate thick prongs. Gwen forked the hay and tossed it over the fence neatly. She is slender, her hair is pulled up on her head in a dark bun.

"You should," she tells me, "just go ahead and have a child and then get married."

"Gwen," Irene says later, "doesn't have time to clean her ears. Sometimes I worry if my ears are dirty too."

Sometimes I feel as if I'm captive to the dead, caught like Queen Heurodis in a fairy world where time is suspended. The hawk poised on the lord's hand ready to strike, the huntsmen caught in midstride, the queen in limbo until Orfeo laughs, breaks the spell, plays his way with a harp into her captive world and carries her home.

Perhaps I will be the one to laugh first, break the spell, release myself from the upended landscape of the dead.

I'VE BEEN TAKING LONG WALKS in all directions. The first week I was here, I walked up to a ridge overlooking Blaenau Ffestiniog, a slate mining village to the south. The dark shiny tailings of the mines spill out along the slopes above the town.

I was walking with a man from home who was spending a few days with me. As we hiked along the narrow shaley path that traversed the slope above a large reservoir, we talked about the precarious nature of love. "I am," I said to him, "a bit dizzy on paths like this."

He was telling me a story about a friend of his who feels burdened with a child. "He wanted to do the right thing so they got married, but I don't think things are that good."

The wind was so strong I was blown over hanging onto the bits of grass growing up in the tailings. We were on our way to a mountain hotel at a pass north of Llanfrothen in Snowdonia National Park.

We walked north to the ruins of a slate-mining village at the head of the valley above Croeser on Moelwyn Mawr, a mountain not far from Irene and David's farm. It was cold. Other hikers were huddled in the shelter of the dark, square stone buildings, polished with mist. The outline of the village is still intact after fifty years of ghosts.

In *A History of the North Wales Slate Industry*, Jean

Lindsay records the misery of men who lived in the barracks where we sheltered, pulled out our map, and sipped water from a plastic bottle. The living quarters were often overcrowded and dank. She writes: "The clothing and habits of the quarrymen were often blamed for their poor health. They were accused of drinking too much stewed tea, and of not changing their underclothing often enough."

We hiked out on an abandoned railway incline at the very lip of the valley, an expanse softened by mist, rock hard under my feet, the delicate cropped edge of the cliff. We were lost and took photographs of each other against the distance that dropped off from where we stood into a series of landscapes to the sea.

My companion went through a painful divorce. He's only just now decided that he no longer loves his wife. He sees involvement as the door to pain. He went on a raft trip years ago, he tells me as we walk along one of the drover's roads, and almost drowned, caught his foot in the lines along the side of the raft and was dragged under the water for a long time. He hasn't been on a raft since then.

Steve and I met him years ago at a party in a hill town in western Massachusetts, near the old mill where Steve worked. Steve and Jim's wife were both graphic designers on a magazine that no longer exists. We talked about Colorado where he had lived and worked with some friends of mine in a ski town with dirt streets.

In the spring, I met him again in the living room of a friend's house. He was discussing his plans for an addition to their house. They had hired him as their contractor.

"Laura didn't know what to do," this man told me. "She

was supposed to be working with Steve, but he was never there."

I'm willing to consider the idea that I might love someone again. I've had to do some violent things to come to this thought. The man is telling me about a barn, about the beauty of the barn, how it was made with local materials, how it was set on sand, how the beams worked, and roof and the doors. Later, we visit a quarrying museum at the foot of Snowdon where two men are chipping out blue hearts from large slabs of slate.

WHEN I VISITED Irene and David three years ago—a year after Steve's death—David urged me to go to the Hebrides. I wanted to go somewhere wild. I remembered that coast of Scotland as windy and empty. I wanted to be scoured clean. I had been visiting friends in Switzerland and England, retracing old steps to help me understand again just who I was.

The traveling was not working. I felt cut off and strange, trying to explain why I was still mourning a year after Steve's death. I walked mountain paths in Switzerland, across high meadows or along the edges of steep hills. Once I walked through a patch of nettles and couldn't remember if they were dangerous or not. I called my parents from a phone booth in a little town. Who am I, I might have asked, what am I doing here?

I took David's advice and caught the train to discover I couldn't get to Harris from there and ended up going across Skye on a bus. Once in Harris I couldn't get an answer at the hotel David suggested I call for a room. He described it as a true fisherman's hotel at the edge of the sea. I imagined Izaak

Walton and his crew, drinking brandy, pulling their wet cloaks off. It had taken me three days of travel to get to the island. I hadn't been alone for a long time.

After a series of calls I found a room in a bed-and-breakfast and was told that the hotel had been closed for years except a bar that was open some nights. I rented a bicycle and set off across the island to the bed-and-breakfast several miles away. The land was just as I expected. Bare, shorn by sea, wind, and sun, the yellow curves of sand set against forests of trees planted by lairds who kept houses on the island. I wanted to look at birds and biked out along a spit of land a man in town had told me was a good place to see puffins.

I rode the bike as far as I could and then left it at a fence, climbed over it, and walked along a narrow path above the sea until I came to an old church. Sheep were scattered around the open nave. I sat outside on a stone, the yellow buttercups, the stiff grasses shimmering, and that sea—open, wide, blue, clear expanse. I was perfectly alone. I had a sense that I was safe there—that my quiet would go out like a prayer—that this pilgrimage by train and bus and bike and foot was an act of faith.

Perhaps the last four years have been an act of faith. I've been retracing my steps here and there. I wonder if remembering my attachments to places and the people I cared about will help me to draw a map I can follow.

ONE DAY I walk to the sea. I set off early so I can take a roundabout way across the hills to Penrhyn and then round the headland across the fields to Portmadoc.

The lane that leads down to the village passes Francis's Wood and then fields where the black cows stand haunch to haunch in the heat, flicking off flies, and the black-faced sheep crop the nubs of grass. Seagulls dip above the heads of the animals. Sometimes a heron flaps up in her heavy grace and moves across the green pastures.

The road passes through a farmyard, the house large and stone, set back, bordered by flowers. Earlier, I had watched the farmers haying for several days, rolling the cut hay into long bundles or scooping it up for silage. After the farm the lane is shady and threads its way to the main road, hedged with thick-leaved plants, holly, berry bushes, foxglove nodding with seed pods, velvety rhododendron leaves that catch silvery light.

This small road in its particularity comforts me. My walk is through countryside that has been pruned. I know at the end of the day I can retrace my steps back to an order cultivated on the ridge above the flats that stretch out to the embankment along the sea. This is a good lesson for me to learn—the persistence of order, the ability to prune life to flower.

My walk is through reclaimed land. The embankment, a six-foot-high bank, stretches for half a mile along the sandy shore at Portmadoc. I learn the story of the embankment from several people. David tells me the poet Shelley had a hand in it. William Alexander Madocks built the earth dam in the early nineteenth century. He was supported by Shelley who contributed one hundred pounds to repair the structure after a storm in 1812. Later, Madocks built the harbor at

Portmadoc, which handled the slate from the quarries in the mountains where I walk.

My route takes me past a church where the sea once touched the stones along the back in a long finger of estuary, almost two hundred years ago. I meet a man carrying a milk jug who lives in the house next to the stone church. His sweater is buttoned once. He wears rubber boots caked with mud.

"I was a pilot on the Mississippi," he says. "Come in for coffee."

Irene tells me later his wife is dead. I pass his pile of split wood on the slippery cow path.

A few miles closer to the sea I meet a man at a shed in a dirt farmyard, metal sheeting covering the barn, where he's been talking to a younger man. The farmer's dog jumps up on me, and I struggle to push her off from my face where she hits her nose again and again. He gives me a ride to the place where he tells me the footpath to Minnforth starts. I remember this man from three years before.

"Some people," he says, "call it a footpath and others don't.

"Now the old ones, they've been using it as a footpath for years, but the council doesn't want to keep it up."

He's a small man and very old, his coat buttoned lightly across his narrow chest. I offer to open the cattle gates, but he says he's used to doing it. His white stone house is snuggled low into the hillside. A tall hedge runs along the side near the footpath. He was cutting the hedge three years ago when I met him.

"The footpath," he says, "is marked on a map I have that was printed in 1800."

He mutters about the gates. "We've been here for forty years and had no trouble and now the man who lived in that farm has given it to his nephew who keeps all the gates shut to vex me. The Welsh are funny, they'll be nice to you and then they'll cut your throat."

He was an Englishman from the midlands who worked in two mines; he came here as a farm bailiff. His wife made figurines. When I first met him, he had been retired for twelve years and complained that he couldn't keep his hedge in shape. It was too high for him to cut. When he moved here in 1947 everyone spoke Welsh, he told me.

I follow the footpath through waist-high bracken, gold flies buzzing in a fist around my head. When I reach the paved road to Portmadoc I see a man on the first bend shading his eyes. He's looking toward the bluff we can see from Irene's farm that slopes down to the sea at Portmadoc.

"Did you hear a siren?" he asks. "Did you see someone on the side in orange?"

As we stand at the side of the road, he tells me his history.

"There's more glare to the light now," he says. "It's much hotter than it used to be."

"You know that cottage on the slope below Cnict?" and I say yes. "My mother lived there and my father used to walk to Croeser from where you are just above there at Hendre Gilian. When I came back from the army my tenancy was up, and even though the landlord, a lady, promised me a holding, there was nothing."

"My regiment came over the pass there," he points. "They've been quarrying that mountain for a hundred years.

I'm still not married," he grins. "The nurse was just here to look at my varicose veins," he says and slaps his leg.

NOT LONG AFTER I meet the pensioner on the road to Portmadoc, I go with Irene to Croeser, the village his father walked to over the cold hills to visit his mother on Christmas. We drive to a house that sits below Cnict in the place where his mother lived. The farmhouse is set against the hillside like the bothy where I'm staying. Jo, the woman who owns the house, has planted a garden on the side. The gate creaks as we open it.

Irene has her massage and I take care of Teleri. I wheel her carriage down the steep rough lanes to the town. When we come back, the two women are still in the other room, so I go into the kitchen where the wood in the stove is burning and rock Teleri back and forth in my arms. I watch the light in the dark kitchen go deep into a pot of roses on the sill.

When Irene and Jo come out, Irene nurses the baby and Jo tells me about the house. English, she's been here for over thirty years off and on, twenty with her parents, who owned several cottages in the valley. Her daughter lives in a house that was her mother's after her father's death.

"She's a hermit," she says simply. Her daughter's passion is to photograph an erratic boulder field near her cottage. She records the boulders in all kinds of light. "The photographs," her mother tells me, "are beautiful."

MY SIN is sometimes despair. Small movements, concentration on detail will fend this off. Thinning the carrots, sifting the soil through my hands to sort out rocks and weeds, holding the bottom of Teleri's feet, hearing Irene call the sheep across the fields: "Anharrod, Meriana, Enid. Anharrod, Meriana, Enid . . ."

We don't swim in the sea on the Lleyn Peninsula. When we go there I walk down to the water's edge across the smooth stones in my bare feet and touch the water. It's tepid and very salty; I can't seem to get the feel of it off my hand.

This is probably the most polluted sea in the world, Irene tells me. But we spend a pleasant hour or so there, eating fish and chips, playing in the sand. Like Wales, I feel as if I'm bordered by a radioactive sea, trouble on the shores, waves washing over the stones clear blue and beautifully dead.

I have a litany of events that clicks on and off. Most of these images are very clear but at the same time indistinct. Still photographs connected to Steve. There we are walking slowly around the block near my parents' house, Steve shuffling one foot and then the other, or the spare bathroom where my father pulled Steve from the tub after he had his first seizure, or the hard texture of the gleaming corridors of the hospitals, or the long weeks Steve called the horrible time when he was having radiation treatments after his operation.

There is no sadness in the touch of the horse's mouth on my hand. His warm breath, the soft velvet of his mouth. Or the tough wool of the sheep as she rubs her head back and forth under my hand.

One day I hold Anharrod for Irene. We tip her up on her haunches and I rest her head in my arms. Irene struggles with her hooves, clipping them, scraping the foot rot out, spraying the tissue with medicine.

"They're quite docile," she says, "once you have them on their bottoms like this."

When she's finished, Irene sets Anharrod on her feet again, and we let her out of the pen to join the other sheep grazing the steep pasture. Trystan and Teleri are up on the hill. Trystan's taken Teleri's blanket and she's lying on the grass screaming. Her head wobbles back and forth like a buoy. Trystan's built himself a fort above us in the crook of a small tree.

WE'VE FINISHED preparing the plots. David goes off for the mustard seed and I continue to comb the soil with the rake, pulling up patches of weeds I missed earlier. Now and then I look up to the buildings—the old farm on the left, white-washed in front, bare stone on the side, the office, all glass where it faces the stream, and the garden where I work, and behind me Francis's Wood, next to the office, Irene's workroom, and then the bothy.

The main house is torn up with reconstruction. Adrian comes at nine or so and makes himself some coffee and commences to pound away at the walls. He runs long miles on the old Roman roads in the hills and is a potter.

"They left the gates open during the run up Snowdon," he tells me, "and seven hundred sheep got mixed up."

Right now a conflict has cropped up over the materials he's using to insulate the walls. David, after many phone calls to the manufacturer, has discovered that the boards he ordered, expensive wallboards complete with a backing of orange insulation, contain formaldehyde. He's decided not to use them. There are two large stacks piled outside of my bathroom window. I can smell the stuff as I bathe.

"All these things chip away at you," David says when I ask him about the materials. He's decided to use some other method and materials for the rest of the rooms. One is already completed.

"We're only holding on in this tiny niche," he once told me.

"I wouldn't have kept on with the job," Adrian tells me, "if they had told me to rip out the room I had finished."

I'M READING a biography of Isak Dinesen. Her biographer, Judith Thurman, tells me that the writer believed that the key to life is to tolerate contradictions. It seems to me that this is good advice. A tolerance of contraries—Peter Elbow calls it embracing the contraries—and isn't that what Buddhism is all about?

Christianity, on the other hand, is always purifying the dross. Chopping the soul clean over and over, flushing out the sins with confession, making the mind new over and over, the body cleared out so it's scraped clean of those complications, those sinful thoughts.

But then again that's the draw, isn't it, at least for me growing up. I could purify myself with confession, get rid of all those bad thoughts, and start all over again. There was still a chance that I could be good. I've just started to realize that being good might not be the point—being happy might not be the point either.

When I graduated from college, I used some money my

Aunt Helen had left me and I went west to Colorado. I had watched a television program about an Outward Bound trip, and I decided that I could use that kind of adventure—controlled and organized.

I thought when I went out alone into the woods that I would learn everything there was to know in three nights and four days. The Outward Bound director told us the solo would be our chance to test ourselves, to see stars clear in the night sky. He didn't mention rain; how often, after all, did it rain in Colorado?

My instructor dropped us off one by one on the sides of Elk Creek. I was the last. My camp for those four days: a grotto of pine and moss and lichen-whorled rocks. My supplies: the clothes I wore, a blank book, pen, ink, matches.

The first day was warm. I was happy to have my own patch of wilderness for a few days, and to think, and wash my clothes and sleep on the flat gray rocks in the river. When the clouds and rain moved in, I gathered my half-wet clothes from the rocks and put them on, chilled.

My instructions were to stay near this section of creek until Bill, my group's leader, came back on the morning of the fourth day. I was cold and hungry. I decided to build a shelter with some fallen pine against the cluster of firs at the far side of my camp. It gave me something to do. Still not dark, the light rain continued.

I learned that time makes no sense in the woods. Sometimes the gray, luminous light of rain and night lasts for so many hours there is no day or week or month. Only the elements that surround each other.

The shelter was a failure. I was cold, curled against the butt of pine tree, smelling sap. I slapped my arms and legs and then curled up again to try to sleep. I slept this way until I thought it was morning and then I tore the shelter apart.

I listened for the first bird to call. Morning always came soon after that, or enough of morning so the sun would inch its way into the folds of the creek beds. I spent hours watching the water move over the boulders of Elk Creek. I walked a path around the patch of ground that was my perimeter to keep myself steady. There was a band of pain around my head, pinching, pinching.

How many levels were there to the river? How many rivers were passing me as I sat brushing my legs with water in the sun? How long had this forest been here on the edge of the mountain creek where elk dipped their heavy heads to drink?

The last night I made a nest of pine branches and aspen leaves. At last I was warm, curled under layers of pine and damp leaves.

I always thought perfection was to be as clean and hollowed out as a curved stone filled with mountain water. That's what I wanted. To be chopped free from the thickets of the body. I was empty and light after four days at Elk Creek, but I was no more like a stone or water or a pine tree than I was before I started.

Years later I watched Steve's father die slowly in a hospital room looking out toward land that was once prairie. I don't know how many days we spent there or what was morning or what was night, except there was light and there was darkness. And there was a holiday that passed while we watched. The room was orange and yellow, we sat on padded chairs. On the last day Rex looked at his watch almost every hour. Each breath was difficult for him.

Was his waiting as timeless as it seemed to us, sitting at his feet as the light changed outside the metal blinds? What kind of hours was he counting as we lost track of days and weeks?

I watched him struggle to both keep his attachment to the things of the earth—hunting and laughing and conversation—and prepare in a practical way for death—selling his pickup, giving his hunting dog to a neighbor, and on that last morning—washing and shaving and eating breakfast.

Steve's hospital room looked out on the city where he had gone to school for a year, and I drove from the Mississippi to Iowa City each day to sit with him. His father had prepared me in a way for the death of his son. They both considered the comfort of those they loved more than their own deaths. His death was not as lucid as his father's. He lost his memory and then his coordination and then his words. On one of his last days I wheeled him outside and we sat in the hot spring sun of Iowa and ate apples. The trees were barely in bud, cars going past, the windows of the hospital reflecting heat back at us.

DAVID COMES BACK with the seed in a paper sack. The edges are rolled over so he can scoop the tiny mustard seeds up easily from the bottom.

"What's the method here?" I ask.

And he says, "Here, take some in your hand and walk there, right next to me, and just do what I do." He scoops a handful up from the bag and lets the gold seed fall between his fingers as he moves his arm back and forth in front and walks slowly down the patch we've prepared. I'm not as good at it, my hand smaller, less steady, so I go back over sections we've already walked through.

"There's enough there," David says. "You don't have to worry about it."

THE YEAR I MET IRENE when I lived in Oxford, I came eventually to a point where I had no words left for who I was. In January I turned twenty. I was starting to recognize my own mind but couldn't figure out what was there. Journals I wrote during that time make hardly any sense to me now. I was trying to describe the inside of my thoughts. By the end of the year I had run out of words. I gave up. I couldn't talk to anyone.

I went home and stayed with an aunt and uncle on Cape Cod in the same place where we used to go summers when I was growing up. I lay on the beach, I started to relearn a few words—water, grass, sand, sky, bird. I was satisfied with just those words for quite a while.

I felt the sensual press of things for the first time in Oxford. Sexy roses, their perfume in my mouth, kisses with a man who later threw me out of his room, strawberries as big as lemons, glasses of champagne, the small sound of the water on the punt as we floated down a river lit by yellow,

cobbled streets that echoed the clip-clop of horses, the early
dawn in May—thick with a northern light, music going all
through me as I sat between Irene and another friend at a
candlelight service, the heat in the hawthorn, black iris
opening their mouths—hairy and large. Yellow lights coming on in the houses those early winter days when I would
walk across the park, touching the tips of aconites, the first
flowers in February.

Now I am soothed by the simplicity of elements in
Wales—sheep, bracken, foxglove, heron, child, mother,
father.

The colors work on a palette of greens and pinks. Someone has made sure the hills correspond to the sea. Nothing
jars from where I watch. I know there's a nuclear plant just
about to close after twenty years. The government wants to
keep it running, but the community wants it shut down. I
know the sea is radioactive, the worst sea in the world, Irene
tells me. But none of this touches me as I sit on the wooden
bench in front of Irene and David's narrow stone house. I'm
not thinking of much of anything except how hungry I am
and how sweet the air smells.

When I was very little I would go to a place we called
the lake, not far from my home in Connecticut. The lake
was more than a long pond—it was a territory of stillness
and trees.

It's the only other place I can think of in my life that
matches the safety here. I haven't been back to the lake in a
long time. We stopped going there when my grandfather
died and my grandmother sold her cottage. By that time Unc

had sold his cottage down on the water and lived in a converted trolley car next door to my grandmother's cottage with a woman who wore bright red lipstick and had a voice deeper than my father's.

My mother hated her summers on the lake when she was growing up because her friends were in town, but it was a perfect place for me. At Nonnie and Pappie's we had to prime the pump to get the water flowing, and once it came sputtering out it was brittle cold and tasted a little rusty at first. At Aunt E's you had to use the wooden two-seater outhouse, and I liked the mystery of that, liked throwing toilet paper down the dark hole. On hot days we would lie on the dock smelling the dead perch washed up on the edge of the foaming little waves. I was afraid of the dragonflies. E told me they would sew up my ears.

We would wash in the lake with old soap, polished hard. On rainy days the fire was going in the big stone fireplace, and I'd take a book out to the porch where there were musty flowered pillows piled on daybeds. I would curl up and read, watching the rain drip through the large trees on the edge of the pond.

MY FEET are starting to get calluses on them. After a week of wet socks and boots, I like this warmth. The dry stones, the rough dry grass, the gravel outside the bothy drying up as I watch. It's been a long time since I was barefoot like this.

Other things happen to my body—my legs pull out, thin down from the walking, my face sheds its winter yellow, tiny lines disappear—my stomach flattens out, the gray streak in my hair deepens. I sleep well. Dreams disappear. I drink a lot of water that has lead in it, I'm told, but tastes like that water at the lake, pumped up in Nonnie's backyard. I stop wearing makeup, my clothes fall into place on my body.

Sometimes I am perfectly happy in my portions of a life lived well. A long walk, fire on my face, cat in my lap, cheese under the knife, stone, heather, fern the size of my palm, sheep cropping the grass, sky, wind, the smell of fire in my nose.

WE SOW THE MUSTARD SEED in the lower patch first and then move to the plot set into the bank below David's office. We are moving in precise geographical territory here. I feel very safe.

Once we finish sowing, David picks up the rake and draws the soil lightly across the surface of the seeds. By the time we finish, Irene has come back from her picnic with the children. I lean the mattock against a tree and walk to the bothy for a bath. It has started to rain. My legs ache from bracing against the pull of the weeds. I rub the blisters on my palms. All through me there's the steady tug of a day at work. My mind is clear. I walk across the gray pebbles to the wooden door of the bothy, flip the latch, and walk inside.

DAVID SPILLS THE DRESSING on the stone. He grabs a spoon from the basket and dips it in the dressing pooled in a depression on the top.

"At least we've saved some of it," he says and scoops the oil and vinegar up, dribbles it on the salad.

We're having dinner on the top of Cai Devad.

"Sheep field," David translates.

We've run up here with two of David's friends who are visiting from London to catch the sun before it dips behind Dinas, the hill to the west. We have smoked trout, lettuce from the garden—thin light green—peas, broad beans, white radishes, bread baked in the shape of a crab—sweet delicious bread—potatoes in a heavy blue pot, boiled on the stove in the house and carried up the hill still in their jackets, an antipasto that John has prepared, with roasted red peppers, mozzarella, basil from his backyard garden in London, tomatoes in oil.

The sun sneaks away from the edge of Cai Devad, soon we'll be in shadow. Teleri cries, Trystan crawls into his mother's lap. Trystan is crying he wants to go home. Li, John's student who we think he's having an affair with, cuts the bread.

"How do you do the peppers?" I ask, and John says, "You grill them until they're black and then let them cool and peel the skins off—very simple really."

"I can't believe it works," I say and spoon another potato out of the pot, cut a piece of butter to roll across the surface of the white skin. Trystan likes the bread and is quiet.

"It's a shame we weren't here earlier," Irene says, "we've missed most of the sunset."

"It's so beautiful though anyhow, isn't it?"

"You know that the ocean once came up to the hills there," John points and I nod.

Teleri rests on my lap. I look into her round eyes, she's drooling, sticking her tongue out, I know she'll soon want to nurse.

I watch John's student Li and think how young she looks. I sop up some of the oil from the antipasto with a chunk of bread. Teleri starts crying, Trystan hangs on Irene's neck. "I think I'll take them down to the house," she says.

"I'll come too," and we bundle Teleri into the snuggly.

"Are you sure?" David asks.

"Yes, I'm sure," I reply.

I take Trystan's hand as we climb down the lichen-covered stones to the grassy patches in the steep field going home. He's a sturdy little boy with sure feet, and we tread our way through the boggy patch where the stiff reedgrass grows and the black cows have littered their cow pats, through the field just hayed, past the washing hanging in the dusk to the house where Irene will put Trystan and Teleri to sleep.

"I'll give them my bed," I say as we pass the bothy. "I'll change the sheets."

"Are you sure?" Irene asks. "You don't have to do this." I nod and she says, "Sleep up in my office."

I climb the ladder to my bed and settle in, perched on the other side of the bathroom wall. I hear John and Li when they come in hours later to brush their teeth. I try to block my ears. I don't want to hear them talking. But all I can hear is the water in the sink, someone spitting, the towel moving against the door.

Later, the slim black cat comes to sleep with me. I sleep well and in the morning eat a bowl piled with red berries.

NELL, WHO LIVES IN THE NEXT FARM up the road, laments the passing of the old times. She remembers when whole families would come to celebrate the shearing of the sheep together. She is as rooted here as Harald is in Finnmark. Irene has been waiting for Nell to call about the sheep. Her husband has offered to shear them.

"We'll have to make a feast if they come."

I'm listening to the sounds of the animals in the field near me, moving a towel back and forth on my head, warm from the bath. Irene has borrowed a few of Nell's black cows to put in the field with the sheep and Patch and Katie to crop the grass close. Soon I hear the sound of footsteps and then a knock and it's Irene with Trystan and Teleri. Trystan settles at the table to paint and Irene nurses Teleri as we talk. The rain has stopped.

My days here have been an exercise in both keeping things whole and accepting the contradictions. Birth and death have harangued me for quite a while—the persistence of loss.

Up in the hills loss is evident all around Wales—the ruins of the quarry, the body of a racing pigeon, torn up, gouged out by a peregrine, only the bones and feathers left, the body still warm. The lost tracks of roads, the art of the stone walls running up abandoned pastures, old fence lines, little green forests, stones covered by moss. Half a stone house here, the ruins of a waterwheel there. A farmhouse, not very old, falling into itself, the bones of sheep.

When I am in the bothy alone, sitting on the bed that runs along the back wall, I often just watch. Late afternoon the wooden-framed window is thrown open to the air. I can see the small poplars in the foreground and the hill behind that—all light green and sky-framed. A universe I can understand, quiet, contained, full of the sound of water.

I have needed to be stitched back into the fabric of the earth. Reconnected first to a landscape and then to love so once again I can touch those threads that connect us. I trust that people I love won't disappear, won't go for walks and not come back, won't get lost on ski trails, won't forget what month it is, how we came here, what road they're on. They will not leave me.

I try, like one of those clever traplike flowers of the bogs, to lure love toward me and snap it up safe, enclosed, directed by my body.

The disorder of these four years has resolved in this place into a whole that I touch and turn and examine. I know, though, that I can't stay here forever. In a few weeks I'll go home, carry my past with me like a shell and deposit it on the walk at Leeds. School starts in September. The garden will be full of weeds.

It's interesting how travel, that suspension of personality, will cleanse the ghosts. Isabella Bird, the Victorian traveler, was an invalid back home in England. But once on the back of a camel or galloping across the high meadows in the Rockies, she was full of mettle.

I like the luxury of visiting. The enclosure of the new. Coddled by detail. Suddenly there are four other people knocking out walls in my memory. The past four years are displaced. Hammered hard against the edges. I almost forget the past here where the stream puts me to sleep and in the morning I hold a baby against my chest, soothe her as she cries.

I become part of the drama of the household. Wound up with the architecture of the place. We hold all this solid by our presence. We move from building to building in a kind of harmony I don't yet understand. The whole place is one coordinate on the map. I don't feel like I'll slip off the edge. I've been colored in here too, another element on the shaded landscape. I can take the chance that letting go of Steve will erase some part of me.

I AM OUTSIDE mostly all day here. Today I watch Trystan throwing sand into the water of the shallow pond where I dip my toes as I read. "You like the water?" he asks in Welsh.

The day is all sheer blue and green. It's just after lunch. Irene has been waiting for the veterinarian to come and look at Patch. After he leaves we try to get the pony into the water where Trystan's been playing but we can't. I am about as far from death on this day as I've been in a long time.

When all the chores are done—clothes on the line flapping, Teleri nursed, Patch back in the pasture, changes in the renovation of the house discussed with Adrian, berries boiled into syrup—we go to the pools. To the beginning of the earth when there was paradise.

I've been to the pools before, but I don't remember that until we get to the top one, a shallow, sandy-bottomed miracle that perches on the top of the Croeser Valley—just on the edge so if you swim to where the water breaks out of the pool, over the lip of the edge, and rest your chin on the rocks there, your body floating out behind you in the cool water, you feel as if you're poised at the beginning of time, looking down the tiers of pools to the valley where trees and grasses arrange themselves in another world, light green, dark green, the sea beyond that, and dark mountains that rim the inlet.

Happiness is a given in this place. The first pool we visit

is the one deep enough to dive into. I admire the shapes of bodies, Trystan's pushing out at his stomach, David's long legs, Irene's skin against the lichen-covered stones.

A friend of Irene and David's comes soon and he pulls me under a waterfall with him to show me how hard the water feels on your head. I'm gasping for air in the cold, slipping on the rocks, holding his hand, his legs, and then his stomach close to my face.

I like to swim up in the deep pool to the waterfall where stiff ferns arch out into the spray. Sun comes through branches and pools in a white light in the froth. When I get brave enough, I climb up the stones and dive in just where the water pulls out in a smooth flow from the breaking.

TONIGHT WE EAT OUTSIDE. A ritual as the sun draws itself farther down, the air cools, the night comes up the valley from the sea, misty, a bit salty. David puts pieces of chicken in foil with herbs and lemon, lights a fire on the ground near the office, overlooking the field where we planted the mustard seed. Irene puts the children to bed.

"This will take awhile," he says and piles pillows in a row near the fire. I gather cutlery, knives with pearl handles, shiny forks, and stack plates on the grass. It's very quiet, no wind, hardly the sound of water. One sheep calls and then nothing. The fire crackles, we can hear the chicken spitting inside the foil.

The children are sleeping. Irene draws her long skirt up under her legs. David pokes at the fire. I am very happy. I draw the silence around me.

"How long do you think it will take to cook?" David asks Irene.

"Cut it open and see."

Soon the chicken is fragrant with lemon and herbs, the vegetables sweet. Darkness, that luminous light here, drawn clear of the sun, comes into the yard. We watch the fire for a long time as the sticks turn their slow way to ash.

9

How happy are the wild birds, they can go where they will, now
to the sea, now to the mountain, and come home without rebuke.
WELSH, SEVENTEENTH CENTURY, AUTHOR UNKNOWN

My mother believes that everything happens for a reason. My parents are Roman Catholics. They believe without question in God.

I've been trying to suspend my disbelief. Something my English teachers always told me I had to do—the willing suspension of disbelief. I am equal to any disbelief I can muster. I've been dipped in the waters of disbelief. What do the waters of belief look like?

Not long after I came home from Wales, I went to Vermont to visit my parents. I ran into Mrs. Harrington, a neighbor who sold a piece of woodlot to my father twenty-five years ago, in the general store. She told me the beavers had rebuilt the pond behind her house on the border of our land. I walked back there to check it out. I skirted north through our woods, culled by a forester this summer, and past the scar where the new house is going up, down the mossy bank to the edge of the pond. It all looks very different. When I lived here alone for several years, I knew each inch of the landscape by heart.

But when I get to the pond and squat by the water, all things become whole. There are swallows dipping above the shallow water and the willow brush along the edges is full of the birds.

Soon, a gray hummingbird comes and dips toward me and then rests on the branch near my face. She's not flashy like her male counterparts, but soft and small, perfectly designed for the suspension of disbelief she's involved in, hovering above the water. I like her calm assurance and the whirring flight once she takes off and leaves me crouched by the water's edge.

I've been reading about disappearing wetlands so this is a small triumph for the beavers to have put the pond back where it once was. The children, Mrs. Harrington told me, have put a boat out on the pond, but I can't find it. I see the prints of sharp deer hooves in the pine duff going all along the old logging road in a deep impression and then the scat of fox, perhaps, and the burrows of foxes or woodchucks along the pond's bank.

I am willing at this moment to believe anything is possible.

10

Still dark.
The unknown bird sits on his usual branch.
The little dog next door barks in his sleep
inquiringly, just once.
Perhaps in his sleep, too, the bird inquires
once or twice, quavering.
Questions—if that is what they are—
answered directly, simply,
by day itself.

ELIZABETH BISHOP

Almost five years after Steve's death, after I decided that I would probably not marry again and had given up the notion of adopting a child, I met Scott. He appeared at my door late one afternoon holding a bundle of flowers. I understood his arrival as something mildly miraculous. We were married not long after.

I had a hard time at first accepting ordinary joy. We lost one child before Graham's birth.

Graham was born in December and Scott changed all of his diapers for the first month or so. I was thirty-nine when Graham was born. Irene and David sent a sheepskin from Wales in honor of his birth. We lived in the cottage in Leeds where I had lived first with Steve and then alone. Graham's chirping in the early morning woke Rachel, who could hear him across the garden from her bedroom window.

Sometimes I traced the blue veins on the perfect oval of Graham's head as he slept in the morning when the sun was warm. I crouched by the side of his bed and felt as if all the world were perched there, new, cut by children's laughter in the playground beyond the window, wind slapping the branches of the fir trees in the clear, cold air.

Graham's first summer was hot. I remember days of one-hundred-degree weather; inside it was close to ninety. We were surrounded by a garden filled with blazing daylilies, their hot yellow centers, the stiff green of their stems. We swam in a pool Rachel installed the summer before. I thought about being forty as I swam—making a whirlpool around and around the small pool. I had read one morning that children were making whirlpools in New York City municipal pools that summer. The boys go round and round until they've captured girls caught in the whirlpool and then they fondle them. Sometimes the girls like this and sometimes they don't. One particular girl was saved by her mother. I wondered if my son would be a whirlpool kind of kid.

He liked to pull the wet strands of my hair down into his mouth as I held him before he went to sleep.

Before it got hot, we had strawberries in the front garden and lettuce in the back. Not that it mattered. I'm allergic to strawberries, but I remembered a night twenty years ago when I was taking care of some children in a small house in Oxford, England. When I arrived, their mother came in from the small back garden with a basket of lettuce and strawberries. She placed the broad leaves of lettuce and the fat strawberries on the counter. I want this, I thought then, to come in from the garden with a basket filled with fruit and greens, my children in the house waiting for me.

That summer I felt blessed with the bounty of my life. The next summer Graham could walk through the lilies in the front garden. He would gesture to the long narrow leaves and wait until I pulled them back from the path. Then, he'd squeeze through.

SINCE GRAHAM'S BIRTH, almost three years ago now, I've been in a body not quite mine. My hair is turning gray. I think about the color of my hair each morning as I brush it, watching my face in the mirror. My mother wants me to dye it. So does the woman who cuts my hair.

"It could be a warm brown," she said the other day. I don't believe her. I know it won't be the same. After years of watching her own hair go gray a friend has dyed her hair purple. Another friend has grown her cropped hair long. It's streaked with gray.

"Someone I know," this friend told me, "dyed her hair and it looked terrific at first, but it just doesn't take light the same way. You could tell that it wasn't real."

"Just don't do anything permanent," another friend warned.

I remember my grandmother's perfectly white hair. I think of her often. She, too, was thirty-nine when her first and only child, my father, was born.

I didn't know her well. I was only nine when she died.

But I remember her hair and how beautiful everyone said it was, thick and white. I have a picture of my grandmother when she was a young woman. She's sitting in long grass and her hair falls to her waist, dark and shining. I wonder if she was vain about her hair, too.

To me she was kind and remote. I liked sitting on a stool in her kitchen with the light coming in through western windows, eating lemon-frosted cupcakes. I didn't like doing what she told me to do.

Sometimes I would watch Lawrence Welk with her, sitting in my small black rocker. When my parents were away, she often took care of us. And in the early morning she dusted my half of a pink grapefruit with a whole teaspoon of sugar. I think I remember kicking her once as I stood by the kitchen sink.

I'm trying to imagine what her life was like. Her husband died when my father was fifteen. My grandfather knelt down by his bed to say his prayers one night and had a heart attack. His father, my great-grandfather, was an Irishman who drank his pay. My great-grandmother would line up with the other wives to collect their husbands' paychecks before they spent it on their buckets of beer.

Nana White worked in a clock factory in Waterbury, Connecticut; her sister-in-law worked in a button factory. They lived in a three-family house on Edson Avenue. She never had a garden. The house belonged to my Aunt Helen. Nana White lived on the first floor in an apartment that was dark in every room but the kitchen. Sometimes we would go upstairs to visit my Aunt Helen and her sister, Aunt

Catherine, who was a nurse and had traveled. I was given ginger ale, fizzy and cold in a heavy little glass.

There were rosaries on bureaus and several crucifixes on the wall, the large kind that opened up to reveal ointments and candles for last rites.

Both my grandparents came from big families. My grandmother grew up on a farm in Connecticut. She told me stories of children who died young or disappeared, like my Great-Uncle James, her brother, who walked away one day when he was fourteen.

I'm reading a book about the potato famine in Ireland and wondering what my great-grandparents' lives were like in Ireland. Did they live in a mud hut and burn peat to keep warm all year? Did they wear rags? Did they know the starving children who had bald heads and faces covered with hair?

My grandmother and grandfather married late, after the rest of his family was provided for. My grandmother adored her only child. And then Nana White was a widow for a very long time. She cut off my father's curls when he went to school. I found them when we were sorting her papers in a large sideboard. She had kept everything.

I'M TRYING TO UNDERSTAND my new riches. I don't remember what I used to feel like but it wasn't like this. Things don't work the way they used to. I am a person I don't know yet.

For years, I had the lonely luxury of spending a whole day biking from my house up to the hill towns, past farms and thick plantings of pines around reservoirs or, when I lived in the West, of climbing up to passes above sparsely populated places where rivers wound their way below me. I could ski whenever I had the time and the money. I didn't worry about what I ate or how often I did sit-ups.

At my college, where most of the students are physical education majors, we abide by the Humanics Philosophy, an incantation of spirit, mind, body. I have a lot to live up to on this campus. One former student is the director of the new Wellness Center.

"That was eight years ago?" I asked.

"You were just a young one then," he said to me the other day when I arrived for my first session with a personal trainer supplied by the school.

I tried to remember a scene with this student where I pushed him up against a tree for disrupting my class, but I couldn't quite prove to myself that it was the same person. Steve had died in April. It was my first year teaching in Springfield.

My trainer is a health fitness major and a writer. The first day we meet he measures my girth. I strap a heart monitor around my ribs and ride a stationary bike. He holds my feet as I try to do as many sit-ups as I can. He is very fit. When I get on the scale and groan, he says, "That's not bad. I weigh about that."

I'm not impressed. He's inches taller.

"Do you remember how to do this?" he asked today as he bent to adjust one of the machines I use to mold my body.

I worked up to one hundred pounds on the leg press. "Oh, everybody's stronger in their legs," Scott said when I told him.

I'm still at fifteen on the triceps extension, but now I

can lift the weights without straining. "Do not sacrifice form in an attempt to produce results," my strength training record card admonishes me in small print at the bottom.

In the Wellness Center I am surrounded by beautiful bodies. I try to concentrate on myself but I can't. I worry about my trainer. I wonder what I look like to him, counting the repetitions as I lift my legs or move my arms.

"Did you read my story?" he asked me today.

And I said, "No, I mean I glanced at it but I didn't read it."

The story is modern. A man falls in love with an actress he's never met but then he's trying to fix his car and the actress walks past him, lean and blonde, her hands in her jacket pockets. She is going into a movie theater closed for years. All the man can see is this woman as he burns his fingers on the engine.

After I finish my workout I feel lighter. I pull on my sweatshirt and stride out the door and up the steps to my car. In the small car mirror I can see my face—expectant, bright.

I run sometimes around a lake, frozen now. This is part of my workout. Yesterday I saw a red-tailed hawk, light brown with tattered wings, wide body dipping and soaring over the tips of the bare branches of maples and oaks. She was calling kee, kee as I slopped through the mud. Two small gray birds chittered and jumped on the gray bark of a tree, buds still hammered shut near the lake. I saw a bush later with exploded buds like yellow confetti curling up from each twig.

SOMETIMES I SEE my grandmother looking back at me in the mirror. She adjusts her hat, dark blue and wide-brimmed, and snaps off the light switch. Her hair is thick and white and curls around the brim. She's been alone a long time. Her son is all she could have wanted. She is pleased and brave.

I am not alone. I count my abundant blessings as I eat my cereal with half a banana at dawn. My husband is flipping pancakes. My son dips his eighth pancake into a puddle of syrup. We all gaze out the large windows at the birds that surround us here in the house where we moved when Graham was almost two.

This morning when I look in the mirror, I don't think I'm ready to dye my hair. I may try to enjoy the slow transformation of my face into someone I don't know well who looks strangely familiar.

11

I made butter—I worked out in the fields, too, all my life even
when I was a little girl. To make butter you set out your milk
and let the cream rise, then you skim it off—keep that cream
and let it sour and then you churn that sour cream. We ate all
kinds of greens. One day he brought me Solomon's seal—you
used it as a soup—you put it into the milk—tasted like peas.
West Windsor was a very friendly town, aren't too many of them
left. I wasn't allowed to go away from here that much. My
mother had twin boys when I was seven—I took care of them.
I brought these kids up. I lugged them around—both of them.
I loaded hay and pitched hay. My sister just raked—but I did
everything. I loved to work outdoors. When my husband wanted
a farm that's what I did again—I worked so hard it seems like I
shouldn't live this long—but one person told me that's why I did.
FLORENCE VAN DUSEN, BROWNSVILLE, VERMONT

The village of Brownsville, Vermont, anchors the town of
West Windsor to a cluster of houses and municipal buildings
in a T on two roads parallel and perpendicular to Mill Brook.
There's a school here, a town hall, a library, a woodworking
business, the general store, the Brownsville Garage, a real estate office in the old general store building, the former
grange hall, now the Historical Society, and, down the road
a bit, a hair styling salon and the post office.

Mount Ascutney Ski Resort is across the brook. We can see the ski slopes from our house. The first rope tow was installed in the 1940s. The ski area has never been big or lucrative, but I grew up there. I was trapped in school during the week in Connecticut but I skied down the mountain each weekend with my family. I moved to Vermont the winter after I returned from Norway and lived in the house where I had spent only winter weekends and a few weeks in the summer before.

Our house sits on the edge of a steep hill that slopes down to Mill Brook. We're right above one of the places where the brook breaks and falls over the stone hunks and boulders of an old dam. A road once came down off the pasture behind us and ran through the woodlot and down to the mill from the first settlement in West Windsor. In the late 1700s, people first moved west from Windsor, where they had settled along the Connecticut River, and built cabins in a place they called the West Parish. The farmers were so busy during the day that they cleared the fields and built stone walls by moonlight.

When my parents built our house thirty years ago, there was an elm at the very edge of the slope, and below that a large old maple tree. The elm is dead now, cut off at the top, the pieces of its branches scattered below, covered with years of leaves and twigs. Along the bottom of the trunk there are mushrooms, creamy-colored collars that poke out of the dark streaked wood.

This is the time of year when the single trumpet mouths of yellow lilies grow in the wet places along Route 44. Once there was a hemlock swamp here.

In Brownsville ghosts are familiar and honored. People keep track of history. Since my marriage to Scott and Graham's birth, I've been longing to claim some sort of place, a history of connection with a piece of land and town. This is the only spot where I feel that tenuous attachment. I go back a long time here.

My past is half submerged. My life with Steve and the years after his death are folded neatly, stacked in my notebooks or the few photographs I kept. Those years are like the stone walls fashioned by moonlight, impermanent but solid, each rock piled against the next in the cold moonlight of the past.

We live two hours south of here in a small town in Massachusetts. We aren't attached to our neighbors by blood or long acquaintance. We rent a house. Some of our dishes are still packed in the cellar, piled in brown boxes near our landlord's old clothes and climbing equipment.

I envy the persistence of families here in West Windsor. Some came two hundred years ago and never moved away. Perhaps I'm staking my claim to a portion of this history now.

IN THE MORNING I can walk down the hill from my parents' house and then through town about a fourth of a mile to the Brownsville General Store. I'm on the sidewalk now and soon I pass two large houses, one immaculate and just painted white, fir trees trimmed like pointed hats on sticks and pots of geraniums by the front door, the other turned on its side, the front facing the side of the next house, boarded up and empty.

When we first moved here we used to peek in the

windows at the kitchen table, cups and plates on the wooden surface, a tattered calendar on the wall. Now a huge lilac bush obscures most of the side of the house facing the street. Next is the old store, now a Realtor's office. The store is where many of the townspeople worked at one time or another and the owners, Swallow, Herrick, Straw, and others, are part of the collective memory around here. We used to buy candy and cheese here thirty years ago.

The store was dark and had a scuffed, oily wooden floor. There were jeans and woolen shirts piled in the back on shelves. When Carl Herrick owned the store in the early 1900s people would trade butter and eggs for grain to feed their hens, cows, or horses. Or they would buy kerosene for their lamps, or salted salmon or salt pork, lace and thread, writing paper, flour, sugar, coffee, tea. There was a pickle barrel in front of the store with sour pickles and a barrel for crackers. I remember the crusty yellow wheels of cheese.

Beyond the old store is a large, square brick house, once the Brownsville Hotel. Return Briant Brown built the tavern with a ballroom on the third floor in the post village that acquired his name in the early 1800s. He had come into town from Woodstock, twelve miles to the north, with a team of oxen pulling a large dray carrying the small house that he lived in while he was building the hotel.

I cross the Hartland Road here, the other paved road in town, and pass Story Memorial Hall where they used to have a Potato Ball in the fall to crown the king or queen who grew the most potatoes that summer. And across the bridge, a few steps over Beaver Brook where I remember a kingfisher waiting on the wire many years ago, his tufted head, his long pointed beak bobbing up and down in the midmorning sun above the glittery little brook, past the Brownsville Garage where the used cars are lined up against the bank of the hill, and the battered green cannon, a replica of a Revolutionary War weapon, sits guarding the establishment, and then suddenly across the road to the Brownsville General Store, constructed in the early 1970s.

Outside the remains of geraniums lean topsy-turvy against the stairs. It's 8:30 A.M. and overcast on the first of July.

I pull open the door and sit down at the counter that runs along the front of the store. We've fled the heat of Massachusetts for the sweeter air here. I'm curious about the way things have changed since I lived here twenty years ago. I still spend time here in the summer, but it's not the same. I don't work here.

Two young women bought the general store three years ago. They've managed to stay in the place where they grew up. The brown wooden building is the center of Brownsville, its hub of sorts. A distinction the store shares perhaps with Brownsville Hairstyling, one-fourth of a mile west, and the post office next to the salon.

Ann Yates, one of the co-owners of the store, has her hair pulled back. Her face is tanned and smooth. She has a grace that extends to the way she cracks eggs for an omelet. I watch her execute order after order with skill and humor.

My companions at the counter are men, some of their gray heads covered with caps, others bare. They are drinking coffee. I order sour cream coffee cake, sweet and moist. I feel lucky to be eating this cake, it's usually sold out by eight o'clock. I press the last few crumbs onto the back of my fork.

This morning is very different from other mornings I remember, when men would be sipping coffee from white unmarked mugs each day when I walked down to the store nearly twenty years ago. The former owners, two men, stood where Ann stands now behind the counter, supplying coffee and donuts.

Ann and her sister-in-law, Amy, have owned the general store for almost three years. They've expanded the kitchen space at the front of the store to serve breakfast and lunch. The farm where Ann grew up is just over the line in Windsor. Now Ann lives in a house that's been in her family for many years. It's a small square house with a large front porch built on the sweep of a field that comes down to the old road that goes to Windsor.

Amy grew up in West Windsor in a red house with a deck that faces the road, on the edge of the mountain. Her grandmother's house is just down the road, a bit closer to Brownsville.

"I wanted to stay here and never questioned it," Amy tells me later as we sit at the round table in the back of the store. She's been cutting up chicken to barbecue and her lace vest is spotted with yellow curry. She rubs at the spots as she talks. "And we both married local boys, that makes a difference."

Her three-month-old son is lying on his back on the floor looking at a rattle suspended above his head. Ann's younger son is four months old.

I tell people I left Brownsville when I was twenty-eight because I couldn't make a living here, but I know that the answer is much more complicated. Ann and Amy could have used the same excuse but they chose to find a solution. Who makes a community? I wonder. Who gets in?

When I left I was tired of living alone. I didn't like my neighbors knowing where I went when I drove down the hill in the morning or where I had been when I drove up the hill at night. I felt exposed and lonely. So I moved west, like many of the young women and men who grew up in Brownsville in the 1800s, when there was nothing for them to do but move. In those years there were more sheep than people.

Now my days here are limited by my job and by my brother's claims to the house in the winter. It's empty for most of the year except in the summer when my parents move from their house in Florida back to Vermont for a few months.

"You moved away," my brother and sister told me not long ago as an explanation for why I was kind of an outsider in the family.

THE NEXT MORNING I run my daily route along Harrington's Road, a smooth dirt road like many around here that curves under maple and beech trees along the brook and then comes out in the open, across the stretch of road and fields from the mountain. I startle a great blue heron sitting in an aspen tree on the edge of the road. She rises up into the sky, her gray neck pulled in, her wings flapping—a slap against the warm air. I can smell horses and the cool waters of the brook, metallic and clear.

Later I walk down to the general store. Everything feels coated with indifference. The shining stalks of wheat, the vetch, the aspens' heart-shaped leaves, the bark of the maple trees, the pavement that begins at the curve in the road.

Last night I started listening to the voices of West Windsor residents on tapes that Mary Fenn, the author of *Parish and Town: The History of West Windsor, Vermont*, recorded starting about twenty years ago. Each voice tells me a different version of the events of the past century here. As I listen Graham calls for water. My parents change the channels on the television. The phone rings.

In her book Mary Fenn lists entries from the West Parish records. I like reading these pieces of history. I learn that "At a Church Meeting held May 31st day A 1791 Olive the wife of Samuel Bayley made a Confession to the Chh for being Guilty of the Sin of fornication which Confession was accepted by Said Church upon her agreeing to Make a publick Confession. . . ."

Hazen Clay remembers on one of the tapes, "In the early 1900s there was a fish wagon in Brownsville, an express wagon with a box on the back. Fish on cracked ice, once a week he'd come around selling fresh fish."

When I get to the store there are delivery trucks pulled up along the side of the building and a bread truck parked in front of the striped awning that juts out over the big picture window near the entrance to the store.

A man and his little boy are unloading bread, "Sold out all that Baba Luis bread," he says to Ann as he wheels a stacked dolly of bread in plastic wrappers into position in the store.

Amy arrives at nine. Three years ago she surprised me and said, as I handed her five dollars for ice cream, "You taught me skiing at the mountain."

And I thought that maybe I did remember her. She was about ten and smiling, her hair long and brown and curly. I was working as a waitress at a restaurant, a small log building just over the bank from our house, although I used to walk there on the road. It was, like the general store, a place where regular customers came every day. For a while we gave water to an older couple who were living in a cabin while their more permanent house was being built. During the day I taught skiing at the mountain.

I liked walking home, late at night, very tired, the air biting cold in the winter, wind slapping the wire on the flagpole in front of the post office or thrumming with cicadas in the summer.

After a few months I got involved with the bartender, a guy people liked but didn't respect. He had grown up across the Connecticut River in New Hampshire. Kenny drank after work and sometimes stayed out all night until he was too drunk to move. People told my parents they saw me with him. My parents were not happy.

I was attached to him, though, and I liked the hours we spent away from work. We swam in the cold brook, or waded up the shallow part on hot days; we fished for small trout and picked wild strawberries on the slope across from the general store. He bought a bike and we went on long rides around the mountain in the green heat of summer. I convinced myself that I didn't care what people said. Later he fell in love with someone else.

As I watch, Ann and Betty are peeling apples, green skins rolling off in round peels onto the counter. Soon the metal bowl is filled and Betty pours the apples into a container for apple crisp. Muriel Best explains on one of the tapes I'm listening to that "My father's apples made the best applesauce. They were yellow and they had a red cheek. The old apples were pippin, yellow bell flowers. There was snow apples—snow apples were red but the meat was just as snow white as anything could be."

Ann mixes cinnamon, apple, granola, spices, flour, and butter and spoons it on the apples, places it in the red stove that fills the corner of the store behind the counter. Above the front picture window there are rolling pins hanging near wide cups, brown, ocher, yellow, green. A pot of paper sunflowers is pushed up against the edge of the windows. This morning the geraniums were gone, the front of the store swept clean.

It was a busy morning, they tell me, and they wipe and wash and ready the kitchen for lunch. A woman I recognize but can't name comes in and sits at the counter.

"How are you feeling, Ruth?" Ann asks.

"Oh, so so," the woman says and moves her hand back and forth.

A man comes in and has coffee and toast. He sits quietly, stooped over the green Formica counter. Amy asks him if he's been haying.

"Finally," he answers and shakes his head.

"They lost that whole field."

"Neighbors used to help each other more then," Muriel

Best's voice on one of the tapes tells me. "Especially I remember silo filling. Usually there was only one cutter in the vicinity. Sometimes the person up the line, their corn got pretty much frosted by the time they got to them. Probably the person who owned the cutter, he had his done when he wanted."

"The cucumber man's here," Ann says.

Betty brings a metal bowl of glistening dark cherries to the counter from the back, "Try one."

Another woman arrives and asks, "Can I make a pie with Bing cherries?"

As I leave a woman says, "Good morning, how are you?" We smile and I walk out the door back across the parking lot and along the street through town to home.

On the way up the hill I meet a neighbor, out in her garden by the pavement, pulling weeds. I've heard from my mother, who has her hair done at Sherry's salon, and from my father, who has his truck fixed at Danny's garage, that Cecil Bascom's nephew is trying to subdivide the land that his uncle left him. He wants to put a road up into the property following the old road that joins Seems Road—right in front of my neighbor's house. When we were here in the spring, Pat stopped Scott and told him that they were fighting the new road.

I ask her how the committee, collecting pledges for the purchase of the land by the town, is doing.

"He won't talk to them," she says. "He won't give them a price."

Her brother-in-law is one of the town's selectmen and

he's fighting the development through the speed limit. Right now the limit is fifty on Seems Road. He wants it lowered to thirty, which would still be too high for another road on the steep curve.

For a long time, when I lived here, I went up the old road, overgrown, barely a track, every day to walk. I remember those late November days when the grasses were gold and the fields just covered with a rime of snow. In January I taught myself the diagonal stride in a circle I skied under the apple and pear trees in the old orchard.

Some days I'd shake the red-brown shriveled apples off the trees for the deer to eat. When I got better at skiing, I'd make the run up the steep hill and into the beech woods silvery and spare in February. Sometimes deer watched me from the edges of the woodlot. I'd ski all the way up to the Sheddsville road, three miles through the woods on an old road and then down through the succession of open fields, now dotted with houses, back to our house through Harrington's woods, past the pond over the hill to home.

Perhaps these are the pastures of the past for me. As I say goodnight to Graham for the third time tonight, he says, "You know something? I'm homesick."

Homesick. His home is a rented house we've been living in for two and a half years, a house filled with light, surrounded by grass and gardens. Here we hunker under trees, and I like that. But this is the first time he's identified with a home—"That is my home," he says. "I want to go home."

For a few years I felt that my home was here, perched on the hill looking across the valley at Ascutney. I could walk all day from here to South Woodstock and back, or up the mountain and down the ravine, cold, a trickle of a stream coming down through ferns and gnarled old trees to the pastures on the lower slopes.

I thought of this territory and house as mine. I never saw many people. There were no signs then to keep me out. After a few years, I felt like the countryside was part of my skin. Any part that was altered burned like a cut.

Now, many years later, so much has been altered. I mark the land by change instead of continuity. I notice who is absent instead of who is here when I walk down the hill with Graham in his stroller. The man who lived in the big white house in town and measured rainwater each morning and told me the results is gone. His wife walks the street in front of her house alone, pulling her sweater tightly around her. I haven't seen Ovis Harrington in the last few weeks and I fear she's disappeared too. The last time I saw her was at the general store.

I have a kind of romantic memory of my days here in this town. As I sit in the general store that memory is eroded. I am an outsider even more than I was then. I am, after all, just watching. I don't live here, even though my marriage license is in the town clerk's office and my parents want to be buried here in the old graveyard near the first settlement in West Windsor.

I will always be a flatlander, born in Connecticut, not married to a native, not connected by history to the piece of land my parents own. As I watch Ann and Amy constantly moving from here to there at their store in the town where they grew up, surrounded by relatives and friends and land they know intimately, the cold waters of the brook, and the best place to pick blackberries, I feel more estranged than I have felt in a while.

But Graham digs in the silt by the little brook. He wants to see where all the brooks go and I show him how the small brook feeds its silvery cold water into the larger brook. "But I want to see all of it," he says.

The sound of the hermit thrush at night when the tractors are silent after haying, all clanking and screeching stopped on the first fine day in a week or so, is mine to possess just as it is theirs. My son sleeps. Behind me the trees on our land rustle as I watch the dusk become night once more.

I SPEND PART OF THE MORNING at the Town Clerk's Office in the basement of Story Memorial Hall, cool and musty downstairs, chairs lined up in the large room and then two offices off that room, just after the kitchen fitted out for big events, plates and glasses stacked on shelves.

I want to find out who owned our land first. The town clerk, Cathy Archibald, shows me the files and then the large leather books where the land records are kept. We start to search for the details. It's a trail of one name leading back to the next. Some of the deeds written by hand are almost illegible; others are penned in elaborate flourishes. I learn that the property we live on was a farm of about seventy to eighty-three acres, depending on when it was owned, that was acquired by Ovis Harrington's father in the 1920s. The farm was open pasture and a woodlot. We're right on the edge of the woodlot in a bit of open pasture.

The original piece of land my father bought in 1968 was described like this:

> *Commencing at the iron pipe set in the ground next to a stone wall at a point 60 feet westerly of the so-called Brownsville Seems road; thence south 30 degrees east 160 feet to an iron pipe set in the ground; thence northerly 86 degrees 30 degrees west 114 feet to an iron pipe set in the ground; then northerly 300 west 150 feet to an iron pipe set in the ground next to the stone wall above referred to; thence south 90 degrees east 110 feet along said stone wall to the point of beginning.*

As we move the heavy land record books from their rack in the vault to a table and then back again, I ask the town clerk about Mrs. Harrington.

"Well you know she had her leg amputated, her sugar's not so good."

A few years ago her granddaughter disappeared on a dirt road not far from where we live in Massachusetts. She was going to look at a neighbor's puppy.

Other families have lost children in violent ways here. One boy was shot to death in a little shed in the center of town after he had run there with his adoptive father's gun. The police cornered him behind the oldest house in town.

I run into a dead end in the records. The property seemed to belong to John and Mary Cady in 1893, but before that there's no record in the Brownsville books.

"Try Windsor," the town clerk says, "they have the records before the 1850s when the towns split."

Another woman, the assistant town clerk, comes out of the inner office. I don't recognize her. She asks me where I live. I give her my long apology for leaving the town. I mention working at the pub and teaching skiing.

"I went to the pub then," she says.

"I was a terrible waitress."

We talk about the land records she's looking at in Windsor. She's doing a project about the old roads around here. I ask her about the dispute over Cecil Bascom's old property.

"There was an old road," she says, "that went up by Rick's sugar house." It's the first time I've heard the younger Bascom's first name. And she tells me how he wants to develop the property into four large building lots. My neighbor told me that he could divide the land into as many as forty lots.

"We're going to have to bring in a mediator. The planning commission and the conservation commission, seventeen people, couldn't agree on anything for that land. And we put it to the town for a vote, and they voted against it the first time and the second time they only won with six votes, so how could we take that as a mandate?"

The town clerk is typing numbers on her computer screen as we talk. I shift one large book off another large leather book on the table. The assistant town clerk puts the papers in her hand on the desk in front of us.

"The problem is Richard Brown and his committee don't have a clear plan for what they want to do with it. I don't want to leave it as just open space, it's in the village— it's not like the land along Route 44. We've gotten that put in a land trust. It's part of a whole plan for the basin. Two towns worked on that. We would rather have vacation houses up there. They don't have kids they want to send to school."

LATER IN THE LONG AFTERNOON Scott drives us to Tribute Park, a grove of pines behind the Brownsville Community Church on the edge of Beaver Brook, one of the little streams that flows into Mill Brook as it makes its way to Windsor and then to the Connecticut River.

Scott stands uneasily at the edge of the stream and I take off my sneakers. We leave Graham's sandals on. He gingerly wades into the cold water and walks from one shallow pool over the slippery rocks to the next pool. I can't resist putting out my hand to steady him. But that doesn't ruin his pleasure at stepping on the brown slick rocks in the middle of a stream. I look up the bank through young beech trees, the sun hitting here and there on the matted leaves of the bank. Up the stream the light is yellow.

"I see a beaver," Graham says. "I want to climb up the waterfall."

"Didn't you climb up waterfalls?" I ask Scott.

"Yeah, and look at this." He points to a scar on his chin I can't see in the sheltered light of the streambed.

Sometimes there's a silence attached to the surface of all the varied and intricate scars. We don't talk about the miscarriage or my first marriage to Steve or Scott's brother's death in an airplane crash. But fear now and then follows us up sunny slopes or into the cold waters of the brook and we reach out our hands to steady our son.

The night I met Scott it was snowing. He was staying with a former girlfriend, her husband, and their children in a part of Northampton, Massachusetts, where a canal used to flow. It was late November. I had come home from Wales and started teaching again. I wasn't interested in meeting anyone. Scott's friend invited me to a party after a poetry reading. I was wearing a long gray coat and a long brown skirt. I almost walked past the small house to my car, but I dusted the light snow off my shoulders and went into the crowded house.

When Susan introduced us, I realized Scott had been sitting in front of me at the art center. We talked that night about all the places we'd been at the same time. He biked past the old yellow farmhouse Bonnie and I rented outside of Eugene, Oregon, in the Coburg Hills. When I was teaching skiing at Mount Ascutney before I moved to Colorado, Scott was working in a bar across the river in Hanover. We had grown up thirty miles away from each other in Connecticut.

As I drove home I thought about him. I couldn't remember his name. He was witty and pleasant. He was very tall.

The next day Scott called me at my office after finally maneuvering his way around the department secretary. He asked me out to dinner the next Saturday. I gave him misleading directions to my house, but not on purpose.

A few days later he arrived at my door in Leeds. He said, "Hold on a minute," and disappeared. He wasn't sure he had found the right place, my directions were so confusing. When he appeared again his arms were full of flowers, the pink butterfly blooms of alstroemeria—delicate but long lasting. His cousin had suggested he bring flowers to appease me since repairs on his car had delayed him by almost two hours.

That weekend we went walking on an old road above a fast, icy green river. I felt as if I were weightless. I liked this mysterious place, loud with the sound of the river. All the difficult days of the past few years disappeared.

After only a few days we knew we wanted to be together. Scott lived in New York City and taught history at a private high school. Often he would arrive in Leeds with flowers bound in paper for the trip. As I drove south to Springfield to teach, I was terrified and ecstatic at the same time. And every time the terror would surface I would remind myself of the unfamiliar joy. When he asked me to marry him I didn't hesitate to say yes.

In January, Bonnie sent her daughter Avery east to spend time with us in Brownsville during our winter break. On the way to the airport the back of my Jeep flew open and grade sheets scattered on icy Interstate 91. We stopped the car and sprinted through heavy traffic as we snatched the wet papers from the pavement.

"This is going to be an adventure with you, isn't it?" Scott yelled as the cars sped past us.

For Valentine's Day, Scott gave me a translation of Anna Akhmatova's poetry. Fluent in Russian, he was familiar with her work. I discounted the suspicions of family and friends who felt that our courtship was too swift. I was still teaching in Springfield and living in the same two rooms but everything was different.

We were married in the summer. We went to Switzerland

for our honeymoon, and I was convinced I would lose him. In Lucarno, Scott hauled heavy green suitcases up narrow streets when we couldn't get a taxi to drive us to the hotel. We hiked across snowfields and I was dizzy and panicked. We ate overdone fish in restaurants on narrow lakes and visited dark churches. Their ceilings were painted with stars and I made three wishes and prayed that we would survive the honeymoon. We kissed near windows thrown open to lakes classically adorned with cypress trees on the shore.

After several weeks we came home and slowly worked out the logistics of our life together—first in Leeds and then in a town known for its hermits. Our first months together I sorted through my past and tried to discard pieces that didn't fit into my new life. Each time I turned up a piece of my life with Steve, it was another stone in the garden for Scott. Finally, most of the photographs and pieces of clothing were gone.

I CALL TO GRAHAM and when he wades back down the brook to me I hold his hand. We follow Scott up the steep bank to the clearing. When we leave the park an older man and his wife, dressed in bright clean painter's overalls, are painting the Brownsville Church that sits above the stream next to the school. They live in the brick house across from the old general store, and I watched him bend over to fill his car with paint and ladders this morning. Sometimes I see them sitting on their long green porch at dusk. Their house was the first store in Brownsville and the first post office.

She wears a big white floppy hat. She hands her husband

brushes and tools as he paints. We nod and say hello, and then get into our car for the short drive up the hill.

WE WALK TO TOWN in a downpour. It's the Fourth of July. Graham and I get wet, but it doesn't matter. When we reach the store the sun comes out and it's hot and humid. There are cars parked all through town, and in the school parking lot and along the road past the church. We're here for the parade. Long ago they were more serious about their celebrations. In the West Parish records, I read that in 1783, on "Oct 21 The Chh voted to excommunicate Dea'n Joel Ely from the privileges of a broth'r in the Chh for appearing to Justify frolicking: and now denying that he ever did Justify it. . . ."

We pick up the paper at the general store where Ann and Amy are working fast in the last of the rain. They've set up a barbecue under the awning at the front, and there are tables on either side of the door. A man tips a red plastic chair to pour the water off and sets it on the ground.

Two young men are carving big hunks of pork, slicing pieces off the sweet crackly meat with long knives. We can smell the flesh in the air. Ann is behind a long table covered with food, ladling an order on a plate. Amy stands at the cash box and her mother is behind her holding Amy's son against her as she talks.

We walk back toward the school, past Danny's garage, where Rick Davis is crooning a calypso song that Harry Belafonte made famous. The red light is on above Rick's head. He sings, "Daylight come and me want to go home, dayo dayo."

And then past a truck filled with wood, the prize for a raffle drawing. Over the stream that feeds into Mill Brook, past a woman in a wheelchair, her hair white and curled, a red raincoat pulled across her knees. Across the lawn of the town hall and past the church and into the playground. Families of three or four kids start to arrive, dogs pulling at their leashes. And a family sits down on the curb in front of us. The three children watch quietly as the crowd converges up by the store.

A man in Bermuda shorts and a jacket, smoking a pipe, walks with a woman with white hair swept up on her head wearing a bright red sweater and flowered skirt. She holds a small dog tightly on a leash as they cross the grass near the town hall.

We hear a band and there it is, the parade rounding the corner right in front of us as we sit on the curb. The bandwagon parks on the grass in front of Story Memorial. The wagon is painted red with golden scrolls along the edges. On the back there are letters that say "Hills Trailer Band, Springfield, Vermont." Their tubas and drums pump out parade music as the cars and trucks and cycles inch past.

The governor is marching, too, and all the various people who want to be elected in the fall. I watch the faces of women. A woman sitting next to me with three young children purses her lips and won't look to the side. Her children are quiet and stay sitting at the curb. Two women with curled white hair and round polished faces sit behind us on folding chairs.

A cluster of five veterans turns sharply on the corner.

"We don't want to go right," one man with wild white hair says, "that would be the wrong way for me, I'm a liberal."

"We won first prize," a little girl shouts from the edge of a float shaped like a pirate ship. Last come the fire engines yellow and red.

I watch one of the men who was marching with the World War II veterans wheel the woman with the red raincoat across the grass. He is very straight, his hair parted carefully. She holds her hands folded in her lap.

THE NEXT DAY is clear and dry, good for haying, and I can hear the machines. On the way down to the store the grasses are chopped and bent against each other lying flat on the field, their dark green and celery tassels faded already to lighter green in the sun.

Ann brings us a piece of blackberry pie with two forks and I take a bite. It is deep red and sweet and bitter at the same time.

I used to pick blackberries behind the house where Ann lives now when her Uncle Perry lived there. Huge berries that were big as my thumb. Carol, Perry's first wife, always had some kind of pie sitting on the kitchen counter in the dim, green place. And the pies were sweet and bitter at the same time, just like this one. The berries leave a sharp aftertaste on my tongue.

I admired Carol Edson, her competence with pies and cows and pottery. I always felt as if I were a different species. I couldn't make a pie crust, I didn't grow up in Vermont, my life was scattered around me. But the days I spent at their farm, I watched in the kitchen while Carol finished a blackberry pie with a fancy crimp around the edges, or put her pottery in the kiln to bake, or picked and hung the herbs she grew, or dressed a lamb to cook.

There was usually a platter filled with squash and apples and, near that, a jar of fresh mint in water. On the walls were wooden utensils and enamel jugs, feathers. Heavy white plates would be draining near the sink. One summer day we baked chapatis on stones in the driveway and ate them hot with sweet butter. And one day there was a man covered in bloody overalls who had just slaughtered some animals for the Edsons.

When I was dating Kenny, he was a good friend of Perry's and he had a garden near the Edsons' barn. He was a meticulous gardener. His bean rows were straight and the earth around them was picked clear of weeds. I helped him garden but never became accomplished at the things that Carol could do.

LATER WE DRIVE up to the Cowshed Road. We walk as far as the place where the road widens and there are several new houses. A man is haying Mrs. Hilt's fields. Graham stands on the stone wall to see him as he swings the tractor with a machine that has the name "New Holland Haybine 477" in big red figures on the side and starts up a new row, cutting and turning the green grass. The men we've seen haying today are mostly older, their peaked caps pulled down over their eyes as they turn now and then to watch their machines cutting and flipping the once-long grass.

We can see the mountain from the edge of the Sheddsville Cemetery, the place where my parents want to be buried. There's a thick stone wall that runs along the road here, one of the walls built by moonlight.

The mowed grasses are mixed with purple vetch and black-eyed Susans and daisies and the lime green cow parsley, all fallen over now, sliced by the blade of big and little tractors. The air is still sweet from the cut hay in all the surrounding fields, along the roadsides, along the edges of clipped lawns. Perhaps I'm more a part of the history here than I thought. We drive past Tommy Kenyon's garden, perfectly clean, the clusters of winter squash plants labeled carefully with a seed packet on a stick. His bean plants are bushy and light green. I know it's time to go home to my garden two hours south, weedy and dry without us.

The alarm for the fire station goes off. From two directions trucks start converging at the firehouse. Jim Kenyon races down Seems Road in his brown pickup and then comes back fast on Route 44 toward Reading. Soon the fire truck follows blaring its thick horn.

12

The shooting stars in your black hair
in bright formation
are flocking where,
so straight, so soon?
—Come, let me wash it in this big tin basin,
battered and shiny like the moon.
ELIZABETH BISHOP

We live now in a house filled with light. Before this our home was the carriage house in Leeds, charming and dark. I like it here in this part of Massachusetts. We're temporary but settled in as much as we can, the owners' possessions still piled in the cellar. Graham likes it here, too. He'd like to stay here forever, he told me the other day. "We'll see," I said. He's four and a half and wants to be a pirate when he grows up.

I'm learning about territory. I've been watching how we all stake out our pieces of the landscape—a train traveling through the valley at dawn whistling a circle around the morning, or a brown cat sauntering across the yard and up the hill at noon, a magpie practicing her songs on the deck in the late afternoon.

It's midsummer now and growing more lush every day. Ripe red lilies in bloom in the garden, lettuce frilled and lime green, oaks heavy with acorns. The wild turkeys, residents here in the winter, come through only now and then in July. We've been watching a young turkey mature with each month, but he still acts like a poult, diving for the ground when the crows' wings shadow above him.

In the winter the turkeys roost in flocks as big as sixty in the backyard, sleeping in the cold trees, clattering their large wings as they settle close together in the branches of oaks and white pines. One snowy winter they came up to me as I spread birdseed from a red plastic bucket on the snow for the chickadees and cardinals that gather at the feeder. I was surrounded by the softly clucking birds half my size.

Sometimes I feel as if the house is a ship stranded in the middle of this old pasture—high, dry, and brittle. Summer storms move quickly across the valley buffeting our house, a rangy wooden tower with large windows and four weathered decks. From our perch we've watched the animals around us come and go and come and go again: a robin who nests under the deck, a woodchuck and her babies who disappeared and reappeared suddenly yesterday, large deer at the end of the row of arborvitae, a kestrel who swoops and kills a soft gray bird every now and then as we eat breakfast.

Last fall a white rabbit with black ears and a black nose appeared in the bushes at the end of the gravel driveway. A man who had come to clean the furnace spotted her nosing in the wood chips. I called her Bun Bun and watched each day as she explored our yard. She was beautiful and spirited, pulling the slim red Russian olive berries into her mouth, or leaping up through the terraced perennial garden, past the clumps of lilies and iris into the shade under the stairs.

I fed her lettuce and gave her water and bought some rabbit pellets for her at a local feed store. Fiercely independent, she survived a cold and then a week of wet weather. I found her perfectly dry under one of the arborvitae shrubs, but she couldn't survive the gash in her leg. We wondered if an owl had tried to snatch her one night. By the time we caught her and drove her to the vet, she was too sick to save.

I mourned her for a long time. I kept seeing her pressed against the cold concrete of the foundation on hot days or sleeping under the silvery leaves of the Russian olive in the late afternoon.

THE ORDINARY ROUTINE of the animals who share this pasture and the woods near us makes me feel more connected to this place. We share our half-acre with dusty gold-and-black striped bees who slip pollen from the flowering lavender in July onto their thin legs, and with dark purple swallowtail butterflies, the hummingbird who sips nectar from poisonous honeysuckle near the kitchen, the large and small frogs in the tiny pond, brown after a winter in the muck and now bright green.

I admire the courage of the animals around here, how they adapt to the changes in their territories.

One year I watched the wild turkeys closely. Graham and I kept track of their travels. He had first noticed them the spring before when he looked out the window in the kitchen while we were eating dinner. Scott saw them, too, and said, "That's a big dog." Graham replied, "No, turkey, lots of turkeys." There were twenty-three that evening running by the window.

It was a cold fall and we had an early, heavy snow cover. Turkeys were roosting together in flocks as large as seventy birds. My father was recovering from a heart attack that winter and the lives of the turkeys cheered me. They were so predictable, so dark and shining against the snow.

In the morning they warmed themselves in the first sun, perched in the oaks at the end of our yard. During the day they traveled their path from the yard across our neighbor's gravel driveway to the next empty lot and into the woods. Or we saw them crossing the road to walk up into the old pastures. At night they lined up in the plowed driveway and flew into their beds.

I drove to the local wildlife office one morning and talked to a biologist about the turkeys. Early settlers described flocks of 200 birds and their beauty, their dark brown color. Biologists estimate there may have been over 38,000 wild turkeys in Massachusetts during the early years of settlement. By 1851 there were no wild turkeys left here. Hunters and development erased the turkey from these small hills and valleys. Wildlife biologists started to livetrap birds from New York in 1972 to reintroduce the turkey into the state.

Supported, ironically, by hunters, the restoration effort was a great success; over 10,000 birds now inhabit the state. In late winter, biologists take several days to lure a group of turkeys into an open field with grain and then shoot a net attached to rockets over the flock. Flocks are trapped in the Berkshires and transported to Cape Cod in individual wooden crates with a guillotine door.

I was curious about their habits. Ornithologists who study

wild turkeys have compiled a list of their attributes: They can survive a week of cold weather without food. Clocked flying at fifty-five miles per hour, they can glide for a mile. Their calls are varied and specific. A gobble is only one of many voices. Young birds call "kee, kee, kee." Turkeys cluck when contented, "putt" when alarmed, whistle, and yelp. One researcher has recorded twenty-eight distinct calls.

Turkeys are survivors; they eat what's available. In the summer they consume grasshoppers, frogs, berries, tubers, and seeds; in the winter their diet is acorns and nuts, and the sunflower seeds we scatter on the snow.

Mating occurs in early spring and nesting in May and June. The eggs take twenty-eight days to hatch. Chicks feed themselves at birth, foraging with their mothers. Flocks might take a trip of five days and then return to their summer or winter roost.

In the spring they wake us at five gobbling and clucking to each other as the sun stirs itself to wake. Their voices are sweet like a brook, different levels coming together in one cheerful chorus.

For a year I kept a diary of the turkeys' lives, or what I could see pressed against the glass watching them come and go. When it was ten below zero I could see the turkeys sitting in the trees or along the old stone wall in our neighbor's field pecking at the snow. They were flapping their wings in the oaks, moving from branch to branch or preening, pulling first one feather up and then the next to clean and oil it.

Sometimes the turkeys gathered in the field instead of the driveway and then at six in the evening took off like magic into the trees to sleep, dark shapes rising at once into the pines as if they weighed nothing, part of the dusk or as if the dusk had wings. We watched them chase a cat away one afternoon, one turkey following another in a line to the woods where the cat ran off through the fallen leaves.

In the winter Scott shovels a path for the turkeys from our neighbor's driveway to the feeder and down the hill by the garden to our driveway. During spring rains they stand in the yard near the kitchen windows and huddle against the downpour. When it stops they shake themselves off like dogs.

In the early spring the males strut and gobble and display their fans of variegated feathers in our yard or the overgrown pasture near us. They dance, the large males chase after a younger bird, flapping their impressive wings and jumping a foot high as they circle the smaller turkey.

Sometimes they peck at the dried seedpods in the garden or stand guarding the bird feeder, chasing the blue jays and crows away. The small birds aren't afraid of the large turkeys and flock to the feeder above their heads, chittering as they knock the seeds against branches.

We have a favorite turkey we call Big Feather; he's often alone or accompanied by a couple of young birds in the summer, and in the winter he's part of a larger flock of twenty to thirty birds. He's as big as a comfortable armchair when he displays his feathers. He has a thick feather, a beard, that pops out of his chest and almost touches the ground as he walks. His feathers are iridescent and buffed chocolate on his back, light brown on his chest. I saw him once down the hill from our house poking his beak into the matted grass of the field. He wasn't startled by me.

A wild turkey recognizes other turkeys and remembers features of the landscape. The local topography is familiar; turkeys know their home ranges. A couple of years ago, the turkeys who roost in our backyard spent the winter in the woods behind us, in a clearing near a neighbor's farm. They adapt to new territory and can reorient their map of home.

SINCE STEVE'S DEATH I've taken a roundabout passage back from the past to the present, from loss to abundance. I've learned to draw a map of home. The cottage in Leeds is only twenty-five miles west from here across the wide Connecticut River, but the distance seems like a continent. Once Steve was gone I traversed the shifting talus that fell steeply to the valley.

The first few months after Steve died I thought could feel his hands on my face sometimes as I sat by the woodstove in the morning sipping tea. Or his left hand steady on my arm as I ran in the woods along the river in Leeds. Later I dreamed over and over that he was alive and sick somewhere living in a room on a narrow street. When I started to concentrate on birds, on the way they knocked the seed against the branch, I discovered how to get up in the morning, how to continue putting the log in the stove. I adapted, after all, like the turkeys in their silky roosts, feather pressed against feather. I live more easily with my ghosts. Now and then I still unearth something from the past—a photograph of my garden in Denver, a card from Steve, a mitten I thought I lost in Finnmark. I try to remember the lessons of the present as Graham chuckles at a story he's invented and Scott fills in the last letter on a crossword puzzle.

LAST FALL I DISCOVERED an old road that continued off the end of the paved road that we live on. It leads past fields into woods bordered by an old stone wall and large oaks and pines on either side. It was one of the early roads in this town. During the fall it was a good place to run—dry, silent. I could be perfectly alone there.

Sometimes I saw where the turkeys went after they left our yard in the morning. As it grew colder and snowed, I could follow their forked prints in the slush up a steep hill to where I could see through the bare branches of the oaks to a line of small old mountains.

We had a mild winter, so I walked on the old road and the trails that led right and left. In April a man who was practicing calling turkeys showed me where the deer had rubbed their antlers on a row of small pines. Turkey hunting season was a month away but he wanted to practice luring the males to him with his turkey call, a small wooden bowl and a wooden stick that looked like a mortar and pestle when he showed it to me. I wouldn't have been fooled. His call didn't resemble any of the sounds I had heard coming from a turkey.

In the summer I started to see litter on the old road—a bag of corn chips, an empty beer can, a condom wrapper. Once a man driving a beat-up little car passed me as I ran down the hill to an open field that has a very large oak bristling with new leaves in the late spring. I wasn't sure what he was doing driving on the rough roads. I called the police.

I stopped running in the woods. The man who lives in the old farmhouse at the end of the street put a sign up that said "No Trespassing." Someone knocked it down but I felt uneasy. This man has a reputation for being ornery.

SCOTT RESPECTS BOUNDARIES. He sculpts the wild parts of the lawn with a large battery-powered weed whacker. He likes to order the yard. He cuts the wild grasses back farther and farther as the summer progresses. His perseverance has uncovered three blueberry bushes that the birds are fond of, a flowering tree, two shiny pines, the woodchuck's den. He's allergic to goldenrod and doesn't like sumac. Yet for some reason, he cultivates the bristly and invasive Scottish thistles that pop up in odd corners of the yard.

I watch him mow and whack as I sit sipping tea on the deck. I won't let him cut a patch of wild grapes and milkweed. We are part of this place. We go about our chores on this half-acre of land, a temporary habitat on the earth as it spins.

Now Graham and I watch fireflies at night flashing above the long grasses and wildflowers at the edge of the yard.

In early May we had a hatch of mayflies. Silvery, long-tailed, almost invisible except for their shimmery light—mating in the air and, my guidebook tells me, dying before dawn. They live a day. They have no mouths and can't eat. The swift-tailed swallows who rest on the telephone wires near the line of arborvitae eat them.

In the center of the backyard is a small pond bordered by rocks from the stone walls that line the property, front and back. Each year I watch the dragonfly naiads crawl out of the water up the sharp leaves of the iris just after the purple and yellow flowers have bloomed and withered into a soggy fist. If

I'm lucky I can see the metamorphosis. A dragonfly emerges whole from the fierce hard back of the naiad. She dries her wings for a few minutes and then she's off—flying above the pond, buzzing her spotted wings.

During the time we've been in this place my son has been involved in his own metamorphosis. He was a toddler when we moved here. I'd have to pick him up so he could see out the windows in his bedroom and his head barely touched the edge of the kitchen counter. Now he can watch the mail truck as it rumbles up and down the street just before his nap.

Graham's imaginary friend, Tiger, lives in a castle on the small porch at the front of the house. She is fierce and loyal and has a band of pirates who accompany her when she travels.

After Graham's bath one night, when I'm toweling him dry with a towel twice his size, he says, "I want to make Dada invisible so he believes in Tiger. Do you believe in Tiger?"

"Yes," I answer. And I do. Like William Blake's Tyger, her shining eyes watch everything. I'm cheered by the thought of her large invisible paw resting on my shoulder.

In the spring Graham helps me scatter the tiny brown lettuce seeds in the two square garden boxes. He remembers words like "determined." He saves wasps caught between the screen and the window. The white-breasted nuthatch eating at the plastic feeder outside the kitchen window is a "seed-breaker bird" to him.

THIS TIME OF YEAR, the midpoint of summer, all we can see is green, those variations of green to the north where in the

winter the hills poke out against the sky. The house is an-
chored by leaf and grass in its pasture and then the overgrown slope down to the farm at the end of the road and the
series of fields like rooms leading in a row into the woods, a
boulder-strewn hill to the north, a wide-open field to the
south. All decorated in green.

We are surrounded by land that was something else, the
whole acreage, almost as far as we can see, once one farm. I
met a man in the fall who lives near here and walks his dogs
each morning at dawn down the old road into the fields
below us. One day he was carrying dried, silvery milkweed
pods. He told me that one man owned and farmed all the
land around us. One morning he was shot and robbed at the
top of our street. His killer fled to Florida. The coyotes get
the turkeys, he told me.

As little as fifteen years ago there were cows grazing
where our house sits. There were hardly any turkeys then,
fewer deer, no eagles or hawks or kestrels. Humans have in-
creased threefold in this town in the last few years. We live
not far from a large reservoir. Once there were several towns
in the valley, poor farming communities forced off their land
by the government to provide pristine water for Boston, two
hours to the east.

TODAY AT ONE when Graham was taking a nap, I heard loud
clucks and peeps in the backyard. From my bedroom window
I could see the sky layered in gray, and below that the massed
green leaves of the oaks and aspens, and then my neighbor's
gravel driveway where two turkeys walked toward our yard,

their necks stretched up straight and thin, their buffed feathers folded neatly in a crease on their backs. A dozen or more poults about the size of pigeons walked near their mothers.

As the hens clucked louder the chicks scurried closer to them. I saw the cat who traverses our yard around this time of day crouched in the Queen Anne's lace by the side of the driveway. She was twitching her ragged tail. The birds that gather at the feeder in the birch trees on the edge of the yard had all vanished. As the cat crept closer, the hens clucked louder like a dull, clanging bell. The young turkeys flew up to the oak trees, their small bodies propelled upward by soft brown flapping wings. The hens walked closer and closer to the cat as she inched toward two poults who were hunched in the wild grasses. The hens' sharp clucking grew louder.

I opened the window and yelled. The cat shook herself, rolled in the gravel, and walked away. Almost at once the small turkeys burst from the trees, their wings popping against the oak leaves.

When Graham woke we watched the procession of hens and their chicks from the windows of his room. Each mother was trailed by a set of seven chicks as she foraged in the grasses and flowers of our yard.

The hens walked down our driveway followed by their poults, soft brown with white spots, to the edge of the bank where first one and then another hen nibbled blackberries. The poults pecked at the ripening berries as they descended the hill into our neighbor's yard.

I think Steve would have admired the turkeys, their numbers, their fancy, iridescent feathers, their attachment to home, their fast flight. He was fond of sharks, their ancient history, their powerful brains. One of our first conversations was about the thrill of things we didn't understand—the sleek cartilaginous body of the shark, a vast herd of reindeer swimming across the harbor at Harstad in northern Norway. And now, even though I can trace and map the activity around our home, I don't understand the heft and girth of the place. I'm content, I suppose, to accept the grace of an ordinary day. I've learned that joy can split itself out of the fierce, hard shell of sorrow.

AT DUSK this yard folds itself around the house lit by yellow lights. My son pretends he's asleep. Frogs burp their lullabies. A tree frog whirs. Soon there is thunder and a pink sky, a few drops of rain.

Reprint Acknowledgments

Several portions of this book were previously published, and the publishers listed have graciously given permission to reprint the following material:

Chapter 1: From "Winter: Kelly, Wyoming," *Quarterly West* 39 (summer/fall 1994), 269–84.

A portion of chapter 2: From "Eldor's Hut," *House Beautiful* 144, no. 1 (January 2002): 32–35.

Chapter 6: From "Exploring the Territory," in *The Writing Path 1*, ed. Michael Pettit (Iowa City, Iowa: University of Iowa Press, 1995), 54–66.

The following organizations have generously given permission to use quotations from the following works:

Chapter 1: From Thomas Nuttall, "North American Sylva" in Ann Leighton, *American Gardens of the Nineteenth Century* (Amherst, Mass.: University of Massachusetts Press, 1987), 63. From *American Log Homes* by Arthur Thiede and Cindy Teipner. Salt Lake City: Gibbs Smith, Publisher (Peregrine Smith Books), 1986. Used with permission. From *A Field Guide to the Mammals*, 3d ed. Copyright 1952, © 1964, 1976 by William Henry Burt and the Estate of Richard Phillip Grossenheider. Reprinted by permission of Houghton Mifflin Company. All rights reserved.

Chapters 1 and 2: From Olas Murie, *The Elk of North America* (Jackson, Wyo.: Teton Bookshop Publishing Co., 1990).

Chapter 4: From Jeannine Hensley, ed. *The Works of Anne Bradstreet* (Cambridge, Mass.: Harvard University Press, 1967), 235.

Chapter 5: From *The Run* by John Hay. Copyright © 1975, 1965, 1959 by John Hay. Reprinted by permission of Beacon Press, Boston.

Chapter 7: From Fritiof Fryxell, *The Tetons: Interpretations of a Mountain Landscape* (Moose, Wyo.: Grand Teton Natural History Association, 1938).

Chapters 8 and 9: From Kenneth Hurlstone Jackson, *A Celtic Miscellany* (London: Routledge, 1951), 103–5, 132–33.

Chapters 10 and 12: Excerpt from "Five Flights Up" and excerpt from "The Shampoo" from *The Complete Poems: 1927–1979* by Elizabeth Bishop. Copyright © 1979, 1983 by Alice Helen Methfessel. Reprinted by permission of Farrar, Straus and Giroux, LLC.

Chapter 11: From Oral tapes of Brownsville, Vt., residents (Brownsville, Vt.: West Windsor Historical Society, 1974–76).

About the Author

Sharon White, Ph.D., is the author of *Bone House*, a collection of poetry. Her work has appeared in magazines and anthologies including *House Beautiful*, *Yankee*, *Appalachia*, and the *North American Review*. She has received fellowships and awards from the National Endowment for the Arts, Colorado Council on the Arts, Bread Loaf Writers' Conference, the Artist-in-Residence program in Rocky Mountain National Park, and others. She lives in Philadelphia and teaches writing at Temple University.